Created TO Worship

Hearts of Love,
Hearts of Sacrifice

D1550846

Norman Jewell and Eva Gibson

ACCENT BOOKS
Denver, Colorado

ACCENT BOOKS

A division of Accent Publications
12100 West Sixth Avenue
P.O. Box 15337
Denver, Colorado 80215

Copyright © 1991 Accent Publications
Printed in the United States of America

ISBN 0-89636-300-7
Library of Congress Catalog Number: 91-70396

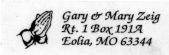

To
Jo Anna,
my faithful wife and companion for 32 years.

To my mother,
Dorene Jackson,
for her faithful prayers on my behalf

and

In memory of
Grandmother Jewell and Grandmother Jackson,
living examples of God's love

Acknowledgments

Many prayed for us and encouraged us as we wrote this book. We would like to express our thanks to those who made special contribution either directly or indirectly to its development.

- Bud Gibson, whose prayers and behind-the-scene support were a constant encouragement.

- Geri Mitch, whose heart for worship shaped this book. She did more than just critique our manuscript. She faithfully and fervently prayed for both of us. Her encouragement was from the beginning.

- Kathy Munger and the worship teams who worked with her.

- Warren Wiersbe and his book, *Real Worship*. We read his book in wonder. Our worship hasn't been the same since.

- Mary Nelson, editor at Accent. Her skillful editing enhanced our writing.

CONTENTS

INTRODUCTION

Everyday on the way to the office I pass a fleet of sailboats moored on the Columbia River. But even though the wind sings through the riggings, the boats aren't going anywhere. They just sit there.

They need someone to release them and unfurl their sails. They need to catch the wind in order to ride the waves.

The God we serve is a life-changing God. A Mighty God. He desires that we experience a worship that will enable us to live lives of adventure and joy with the Wind of God singing through our rigging, filling the sails of our lives.

But how do we do it? How do we open our hearts so that we catch the wind? The mighty Wind of God?

That's why we wrote this book. More than anything we want you to experience a worship that will transform your life.

SECTION ONE/
WHO ARE YOU, LORD?

Chapter One/
I Am The One Who Brings
Beauty Out of Chaos

Many Christians long to obey God's Word, pray without ceasing, and experience the joy of worship and service.

Instead, the baby cries all night. The lawn grows more dandelions than it does tender new grass. The electric bill is past due; the garbage needs to be taken out, and the phone won't stop ringing.

Carla, a woman with four almost grown children, cries out, "Nothing is the way I thought it would be. Nothing!

"Rick hates his job. He's depressed and angry all the time. And I'm so tired. I get up at 5:00 in the morning and work on an assembly line all day.

"We never have meals together anymore. It's a sandwich on the run, a quick, 'See you later, Mom. I've got to go.'

"I never have time for myself—much less time for worship. I've lost something beautiful and good and I don't know how to find it.

11

"I need to get back to God, but I don't know how."

Most of us, if we're honest, can identify with Carla. Can we really participate in a life that is greater than we are? Can we learn to worship God when darkness clouds our thoughts and our lives fall into confusion? When our senses tell us to run after pleasure and enjoyment instead of Him? Is joy really possible in spite of raw ordinariness and the sheer pain of existence?

Yes. But real worship can only come as we focus on God and who He is.

Let's go back to the beginning.

The Breath of Almighty God

God the Creator takes the stage in the first verse of Genesis: "In the beginning God created the heavens and the earth."

The second verse shows the Holy Spirit as Co-Creator. He hovers over the earth's deadness, moves above shrouded, chaotic confusion. He is the very breath of God.

His breath forms a command, "'Let there be light,' and there was light."

Herbert Lockyer[1] writes, "Light would not have made those waters good and glad, if the Spirit of Light had not first moved upon them. There would not have been the herb of the field, the bird of the air, the fish of the sea, the masterpiece of man, if the brooding Spirit had not acted first. The Spirit came before all His gifts—before the light, before the firmament, before all the beauty and provision of nature. First of all, He moved upon the shapeless face of the water, and then came light with its charm, the herb with its greenness, and the bird with its song."

We do well to seek to know Him for He precedes all things. Though invisible, He is the energy of creation, the very breath of the Almighty. "The Spirit of God has made me; the breath of the Almighty gives me life" (Job 33:4).

"My Baby, My Baby"

One of the most significant moments of my life was to be present when my granddaughter, Jewel Ann, made her entry into this world.

When my children were born, it was the custom to send the father into the waiting room to read magazines. I must have leafed through every page of every magazine the hospital had in that room as I sat—alone—waiting for word of my child's birth.

But times have changed. Not only are husbands allowed to be present during birth, other family members are permitted to be there as well.

April 1, 1988—my son-in-law, Brad, and I stood beside my daughter, Debbie, in a California hospital. Delivery was imminent—I couldn't help but think about the miracle of new birth.

For nine months this little life, so soon to be born, had been surrounded by fluid. For nine months it had floated in protected warmth and darkness, close to my daughter's heart.

Then...within a matter of seconds, a dramatic change took place. The tip of our baby's head appeared, no bigger than a dime.

Debbie cried out and pushed with all her might. The baby's entire head emerged...then the shoulders.

My granddaughter burst into the world...and took her first breath.

The wonder of that moment defies words. Perhaps it's best expressed in my daughter's cry of joy, "My baby, my baby," as the doctor placed her naked, squirming daughter on her stomach.

I marveled as I touched Jewel Ann's tiny feet and watched her little chest move up and down. This little girl's life would never again be the same. No longer would she need to be sustained through the umbilical cord. The Almighty God had breathed into her the breath of life.

13

Heart To Heart

There is something beautiful about the breath of the Almighty. Even His name, the Holy Spirit, carries the idea of moving, vitalizing breath.

The word God used to describe the Bible, inspiration, means "God-breathed" (II Timothy 3:16). And the breath of the Almighty takes the thoughts of God and gives them voice. Throughout the Old Testament we hear the phrase, "the Spirit of God saith." Without the Spirit we wouldn't have the Word of God. We wouldn't be able either to know God or to understand His heart.

The Holy Spirit knows how to take thoughts we can't express, translate them into heavenly words, and carry them straight to the Father. It is by the Spirit we cry, "Abba, Father" (Romans 8:15). It is the Spirit who helps us in our weakness. "We do not know what we ought to pray, but the Spirit himself intercedes for us with groans that words cannot express" (Romans 8:26).

The depths of God's heart call to the deep places within the hearts of His children. "Deep calls to deep in the roar of your waterfalls; all your waves and breakers have swept over me" (Psalm 42:7).

"By day the Lord directs his love, at night his song is with me—a prayer to the God of my life" (Psalm 42:8).

The deep, hidden places inside us resonate with a quickening, our response to our Creator.

The Holy Spirit brings God's heart and our hearts together. He makes communication between the two of us possible.

Our response needs to be one of worship.

Worshiping Our Creator

The first of the four worship songs in Revelation is of adoration to God as Creator of the universe. The heavenly hosts are singing (4:8,11):

14

"Holy, Holy, holy,
is the Lord God Almighty,
who was, and is, and is to come...."
You are worthy, Our Lord and God,
to receive glory and honor and power,
for you created all things,
and by your will they were created
and have their being."

Why is it important to worship Him as the God of Creation? Unless we first recognize that we are answerable to a Creator, we'll never see that we are sinners in need of a Redeemer, never recognize our need to bow humbly before a God who has the power to forgive sin.

Without knowledge of God as Creator, we are blind to the real beauty and wonder of His creation. Our hearts cannot sing, "The heavens declare the glory of God; the skies proclaim the work of his hands" (Psalm 19:1). Somehow we aren't able to connect the Creator and creation.

When we do connect the two, we discover a deepening joy. A baby's fingers wrap around our own; we bite into an icy watermelon on a hot day; we discover an unexpected flower blooming in a desert. Our spirits are moved.

We also need to respond by allowing God to still our hearts, give us a song, or deepen our adoration as we stand shoulder to shoulder with others in corporate worship.

When we allow these experiences to imprint our lives, they teach us more about what it means to reverence and adore our Lord.

Beauty Out of Ugliness
A Creator God has the power to give us hope. He is a faithful Creator (I Peter 4:19) and a faithful Creator who makes "all things work together for good to them that love God" (Romans 8:28, KJV).

15

A creative God can bring order out of chaos and transform ugliness into beauty. He promised He would provide for those who grieved in Zion, "...a crown of beauty instead of ashes, the oil of gladness instead of mourning, and a garment of praise instead of a spirit of despair" (Isaiah 61:3). A friend of mine tells how an old pickup and a load of garbage illustrated God's power to transform the ugliness in her life and the lives of others into beauty:

"My husband parked an ancient pickup in the backyard, just outside the kitchen window. He told me and the kids to throw all our garbage and discards into it, and he'd drive it to the dump.

"It didn't take us long to fill that old pickup with smashed plastic jugs, rusted pipes and cans, tattered clothes, crushed cardboard....

"And then...that old pickup wouldn't start.

"And so it sat.

"For months, every time I prepared meals or cleaned the kitchen, I'd look out the window and see that dented pickup with its ton of garbage. I hated the sight—the disorderly ugliness grated my spirit.

"Winter came and one night it snowed. I went into the kitchen to make hot chocolate and someone turned on the porch light. I looked out the window.

"Huge snowflakes drifted down and light reflected off the pickup windows. Ugly cans, frayed sponge rubber, a rusted mattress, all were frosted in an intricate design of white fringed with black.

"It made me want to cry. That old, ugly pickup with its mess of garbage had been transformed into beauty.

"I'll never forget that picture of God's grace. That night He showed me in a new way His power to transform ugly circumstances and situations into beauty.

"Since then I've seen Him do the same for people who've been bruised and scarred by sin. I've cried with young girls still hurting over the decision they'd made to abort their babies, been there when God poured in His comfort. I've watched Him tenderly transform their pain into a compassion that eventually enabled them to reach out to other hurting women.

"How does God do it?

"I don't know. I only know He does."

Old Bones Made New

A boy abused by his stepfather, a man hurting over the loss of a job, a woman weeping over an adolescent child who's making wrong choices. Israel's cry in the valley of dry bones could well be their own, "Our bones are dried up and our hope is gone; we are cut off" (Ezekiel 37:1-14).

The winds blow. Ezekiel hears the rattling as the bones come together, "bone to bone." He watches tendons and flesh appear, then skin to cover them.

Then words of hope. "This is what the Sovereign Lord says: Come from the four winds, O breath, and breathe into these slain, that they may live." Breath enters them at the Word of the Lord.

The bones stand on their feet—a vast army.

Our powerful Creator God had power to breath life into those old bones. The Wind of His Spirit reveals, more clearly than any other symbol, God in action.

The Wind

It is significant that both the Hebrew word for spirit, *ruach*, and its Greek equivalent, *pneuma*, mean "wind" or "breath." There are striking similarities between the winds of earth and the movement of the Holy Spirit. Neither the wind nor the Spirit can be controlled by mankind. Neither the wind nor the Spirit are visible or predictable. But both are powerful—the results of both clearly seen.

Listen to Jesus explain to Nicodemus the wonder of spiri-

17

tual birth. "The wind blows wherever it pleases. You hear its sound, but you cannot tell where it comes from or where it is going. So it is with everyone born of the Spirit" (John 3:8). Sometimes the wind comes without warning, a mighty force uprooting trees and tossing roofs. On the day of Pentecost, the Spirit came "like the blowing of a violent wind...from heaven" (Acts 2:2). Herbert Lockyer says it suggests, "...the irresistible action of the Spirit."[2]

The Holy Spirit revealed Himself when He lifted Ezekiel up between the earth and heaven (Ezekiel 8:3); when He caught Philip away, removing him from one place and setting him down in another (Acts 8:30-40).

It is possible for the Holy Spirit to drive, lift, and control without our wills involved, but He doesn't often choose to do so. More often He comes as the breath of God, with the softness of falling snow.

Setting the Sail

We can't expect God's Spirit always to act in the same way. He came to Christ's tomb with earthquake power...and the keepers fell to the ground as dead men. He opened Lydia's heart with quiet gentleness, and the door to her household and that of the continent of Europe swung wide.

We serve a creative God. An energizing, life-giving God who desires to change our lives and lift us into worship.

But we have a responsibility.

A boat bobs on the sparkling blue water of the Willamette River. It's afloat all right. But it's just sitting there, bobbing restlessly on the sparkling water. The sail must be hoisted to catch the wind before the boat can ride the waves.

That boat might be a little like you. You're waiting, longing to move out onto the waters. But you don't quite know how to hoist the sail. You don't know how to cooperate with the wind so that you move in a direction that will send you skimming across the waves.

18

God has something more for you than a stoic setting of one foot in front of the other. He designed you to live a life of adventure and joy; He longs for you to experience a worship that results in a transformed life. He wants you to run with the wind...the Wind of God.

FOOTNOTES

[1]Taken from the book, *All the Divine Names and Titles in the Bible* by Herbert Lockyer. Copyright © 1975 by The Zondervan Corp. Used by permission.

[2]*Ibid.*

19

Helps in Setting the Sail:
1. Read Psalm 104. Use the imagination God gave you to savor each verse. Capture the wonder of your God wrapped in light, riding on the wings of the wind. Listen for the thunder of His voice.

2. Meditate on the worship seen through the open door of heaven in Revelation 4. Allow the heavenly scene to catch at your spirit. Make the words the living creatures sing your own personal worship song. Sing it to the One sitting on the throne.

Suggestions for Family Sailing:
Jesus said, "Let the children come to Me."
Let's make it fun for them to come.

1. Plan a picnic by the sea...or a stream or on a hillside. Bring an unsliced loaf of bread, chunks of cheese, apples and raisins (leave the silverware at home). Pick wildflowers and look at them like lilies of the field. Read parts of Jesus' Sermon on the Mount (Matthew 5–7) as you break the bread and munch your meal.

2. Challenge your child to discover a "new creation" today. And don't forget to look for one yourself! Hint: It could be a new flower, a new thought about God, or even a new situation.

3. Buy a kite and head for an open area. Read Psalm 148:7-10. Emphasize the "small creatures and flying birds" in verse 10. Hoist your kite and run with the wind! Feel its tug and the exhilaration of running with it.

4. Have a sit-down meal with your family. Make it special with flowers and candles or by getting out the pretty china, napkins and silverware.

Choose verses from Psalm 104 and read them. Challenge each person to think about their Creator God by closing their eyes and putting the verse into a picture. Have each of you share your word picture with the family. You may even be encouraged to get out crayons or water colors and practice transforming your thoughts into a drawing.

Chapter Two/
I Am the Shepherd and the Lamb

The afternoon is a perfect one to spend at the Willamette River Waterfront in Portland, Oregon. The sky is cloudless, a soft breeze ruffles my hair.

My wife Jo Anna and I scatter crumbs. We watch as several birds cluster to peck at our small offering. "All we need is a chipmunk or two," Jo Anna observes.

I smile. But my attention is really on the moored sailboat riding the water. Its bare rigging almost seems to cry for a lifted sail, the fresh blue paint to shout, "I'm ready to ride the waves. Please. Let me go with the wind."

Several boats, white sails puffed with wind, glide past. Their bows dip starboard, then lilt upward. Their rigging hums with the song of the wind. Waves slap their sides. They're skimming over the water, moving forward.

Eagerly, almost longingly, the moored boat lifts its bow, tugs restlessly at the rope holding it to the shore.

Something stirs in me.

I remember another day when the wind blew. The sailboat

beneath my feet had responded to the touch of my hand on the rudder. The sails had swelled, filled with a power not their own. The boat leaped forward. Although I was only going 3 or 4 knots, it felt like 50 mph in the back of a pickup truck. The bow sliced through the waves. An intense joy consumed me as I concentrated on directing the boat with the shift of the sail and the turn of the rudder.

It was like flying and I—I was an eagle freed from a cage, riding the air currents, dipping, soaring.

I was freed to fly...to soar....

Freed to Worship

There are few things in life that compare with sailing a boat on a day when the air is alive with movement and the sun sparkles the water. It can only be likened to the joy that comes when we're freed to worship, to express unashamedly the presence and the moving of the Holy Spirit in our lives.

This joy and freedom comes when we're under the influence of the Spirit's control. Perhaps it is best expressed in Peter's words, as, "joy unspeakable and full of glory" (I Peter 1:8, KJV).

This unique joy, so difficult to describe with words, can only be experienced through a personal relationship with Jesus.

The sailboat tied to the mooring is a picture of those who have committed their lives to Christ but seldom experience the joy of worship. Though they long for freedom, their hearts are tied to the here-and-now, and they can't participate in a joy beyond their human limitations. No matter how they try to satisfy the deep longings inside, they're unable to do more than bob restlessly on the sea of life.

They need to be restored, to hear again redemption's song. That song is the song of the Shepherd, the song of the Lamb.

23

The Shepherd Who Became the Lamb

Jesus is referred to as "the Lamb" twenty-eight times in the book of Revelation. How can our Creator God be both ruler and redeemer? Both the Shepherd and the Lamb? "I have come that they may have life, and have it to the full. I am the good shepherd. The good shepherd lays down his life for the sheep" (John 10:10-11). Jesus declares the "how" for those who will listen.

David knew God as the Good Shepherd. He knew from personal experience what it was like to grapple with disappointment, rejection, sin, and sorrow. Through all those things he discovered God's goodness. He could say, "You are with me."

In no other name is the closeness and intimacy God desires to have with us more beautifully expressed than in David's words, "The Lord is my shepherd."

Isaiah knew God as the Great Shepherd. In chapter 40 he paints a picture of his great and powerful God. And then, right in the middle, he interjects these words in a single verse: "He tends His flock like a shepherd: He gathers the lambs in his arms and carries them close to his heart; he gently leads those that have young" (Isaiah 40:11).

Peter knew Christ as the Chief Shepherd (I Peter 5:4). He knew His goodness before he understood His greatness. He recognized His greatness before He made Him his chief.

Jesus became the Good, Great, and Chief Shepherd by becoming a lamb. As the Shepherd, he identified Himself so totally with us, His sheep, that He became the Lamb of God who takes away the sin of the world (Isaiah 53:5-7; John 1:29, 10:11).

The two disciples who were closest to Christ while He was on earth saw Him as that Lamb. John recognized Him as the newly slain Lamb; Peter understood that He was ordained to shed His blood before the world began.

We see Christ as both the Shepherd and the Lamb in

Revelation 7:17. "For the Lamb at the center of the throne will be their shepherd; he will lead them to springs of living water. And God will wipe away every tear from their eyes."

Listen to the song the elders sing to the resurrected Lamb, the Savior of the world (Revelation 5:9-12). It is the new song that only the redeemed can sing.

"You are worthy to take the scroll
and to open its seals,
because you were slain,
and with your blood you purchased men for God
from every tribe and language and people and nation.
You have made them to be a kingdom
and priests to serve our God,
and they will reign on the earth....
Worthy is the Lamb, who was slain,
to receive power and wealth and wisdom and strength
and honor and glory and praise!"

The Lamb who is the Shepherd is worthy of our worship. He was slain, the perfect Lamb at Calvary.

Before that?

Gethsemane—"The place of great crushing"

The name Gethsemane signifies an oil press. And the Lord Jesus Christ, the One who created the world, did not escape its bruising. Here in His bitterest hour, He wept—alone—the good Shepherd, the Great Shepherd—wrestling with the sin of the world.

That night He looked into the ugly cup of sin. He looked, then touched it to His lips.

Leonard Ravenhill describes the cup in his article, "The Husbandman," in *The Message of the Cross:*

"Crystallized in that cup was all the sin of man. Mirrored in its depths was the ultimate in human depravity. Jesus did not

25

step back from that bitter cup. He drank its dregs."

Because He drank that cup and shed His blood, we can, by believing and asking for His forgiveness, sing Redemption's Song in perfect harmony with all the saints. It is a song only those who've been cleansed by the blood of the Lamb can sing.

Lost Joy

Why then do we who've experienced His cleansing, who call ourselves Christians, fail to sing it?

A young woman sits in my study, her hands cover her face. I have to lean forward to hear her whisper, "I've lost the joy of my salvation. I don't know how to get it back."

Her marriage is falling apart. "It's all my fault. I let my anger grow into bitterness—resentment—hate. I wouldn't forgive. My love died."

Her friendship with God is severed. "I can't pray. I don't even want to. And my Bible just sits there on the table. I can't force myself to open it, let alone read it."

This woman needs to learn Confession's Song. She needs to personalize to her own heart the words David sang in Psalms 51 and 32.

When Confession Becomes Worship

"Have mercy on me, O God, according to your unfailing love; according to your great compassion blot out my transgressions" (Psalm 51:1).

Lord Jesus, I need you. I've sinned.

I've been angry, God. I haven't known how to handle the disappointment I feel over what you've said you'd do—except you haven't.

"When I kept silent, my bones wasted away through my groaning all day long. For day and night your hand was heavy upon me; my strength was sapped as in the heat of summer" (Psalm 32:3-4).

26

I've held in my anger for a long time. It's lain inside, festering, become a bitter root that's slowly drained me of energy. My love that once was so fervent for you and for your people has become dull, lukewarm. It's almost like I don't care anymore.

Lord, I need a new heart.

"Cleanse me with hyssop, and I will be clean; wash me, and I will be whiter than snow. Let me hear joy and gladness; let the bones you have crushed rejoice" *(Psalm 51:7-8).*

I lay before you my sin, my own crushed and broken spirit. *"Restore to me the joy of your salvation"* *(Psalm 51:12).*

I love you, Lord—I worship you.

Worship Leads to Restoration

Confession and worship go together. Restoration follows them.

Let's look at a dramatized scene of restoration in Zachariah 3. The setting is heaven.

Joshua, the high priest, is there, and he's in desperate condition. He stands before the angel of the Lord, Jesus Himself. Satan, his enemy, is at Joshua's right hand ready to accuse him. Others with Joshua are his fellow believers and Zachariah—prophet, witness, and recorder. God the Father surrounds the scene and Jesus supervises.

Satan hisses ugly words into Joshua's ear. "You're a mess, Joshua. You say you're a priest of God? That you want to be His servant? You think He has a plan for you? Joshua, you've got to be kidding!

"You're a sinner. All you ever will be is a sinner. Why, you've failed at everything you've ever tried."

He laughs loudly so everyone can hear. "All you have to do is look back at this past year. Just look at it. How can you tell anyone else how to live? You can't live a godly life no matter

27

how you try. Even your clothes are filthy."

Satan's voice gentles. "Joshua, you've disqualified yourself. Why don't you do the wise thing? Forget this High Priest business. Chuck the whole thing. Go try another line of work, one for which you're better suited.

"Why, Joshua, with you into something better, I'd get off your back. You could have peace again."

Satan turns to those around the throne. "Let Joshua's own thoughts condemn him. He is a sinner. A failure to God. A failure to the temple. A failure to his own self. Let him find a hole to crawl inside. Let—"

The voice of God thunders through the heavens. "The Lord rebuke you, Satan! The Lord, who has chosen Jerusalem, rebuke you! Is not this man a burning stick snatched from the fire?"

Restoration By God's Own Hand

God says to all of heaven, "I have chosen this man. My glory dwells in him. He is mine. Take off his filthy clothes."

He turns back to Joshua. "See, I have taken away your sin. You've been cleansed of your filthiness. Now your fellow believers will clothe you in my righteousness."

Zechariah, the silent watcher, can keep silent no longer. "Put a clean turban on his head!" In other words, "Let God's joy flow through him like a river, bring to him a fresh, clear stream of pure life and restoring thoughts."

Joshua's fellow believers place the turban on his head. Then the Lord Almighty says to Joshua, "Nothing you have done in yourself merits the position I have given you." God explains. "All you have is a result of my love and mercy. You are mine and you will be holy to me." Then He says, "Walk in my ways and keep my requirements, then you will govern my house and have charge of my accounts, and I will give you a place among these standing here."

Restoration—from the lips of God Almighty to everyone

who will keep His requirements.

There is a beautiful principle in Joshua's story—God always restores those who turn from sin and reach out to Him. David knew this. We find the same principle captured in Psalm 23. We hear David's quiet assurance, "He restores my soul."

Even though failure is inevitable for all of us, our God still reaches out in love. He does it even though he knows that if we're going to walk, we're going to fail. If we're going to live, we're going to sin. But no matter what we've done, God always restores those who come back to Him. God never holds grudges. Indeed, He forgets we ever sinned against Him (Isaiah 43:25).

Restoration is similar to repentance. We're responsible to turn from what cast us down and move in the opposite direction.

Our God never intended that we be moored, tied, a victim of sin and circumstances. He wants more for us than a frustrated bobbing up and down.

He longs to fill us, to hear us say, "Lord, here I am. Take possession." We belong to Him and He is willing to do that, just as light is willing to flood a room if only it is opened to its brightness.

We're created to worship, to lift our hearts in joyous abandon to His Spirit. If you feel like an empty channel of that miraculous love, open the floodgates. He'll flow in and fill you.

29

Helps in Setting the Sail:
1. Perhaps writing down the sins weighing on your heart will help you rediscover joy. A fireplace is a good place to burn them in. There's something freeing about watching the things that have shackled you go up in smoke.

2. Take your Bible and go to a quiet place where you can worship God. Create your own prayer of confession using Psalms 32 and 51 as models. Write down a verse, then follow it with a personal response. Express your new song outloud to your Lord. If it sounds strange to your ears, whisper instead. Either way, He'll delight in your song.

Suggestions for Family Sailing:
1. Children need to experience the joy of forgiveness, to know what it means to be redeemed. Encourage them to do the writing exercise in #1 of *Helps in Setting the Sail.*

It can be even more meaningful if it can be part of a family trip to a quiet place outdoors. Find a place to build a fire, and burn your papers while you read Micah 7:18-19; Psalm 103:11-12; I John 1:9. Talk about God as a consuming fire who has power to consume the sin in your lives (Hebrews 12:28-29).

2. Take a "Restoration" ride together. Look for signs of a devastation: a recent fire, logged area, landslide, downed tree. Then look for renewal: reforestation project, new life on a landslide, a mother log sprouting moss, ferns, tiny trees.

Mt. St. Helens in Washington is a parable of restoration. Devastated by a volcano blast May 18, 1980, it is gradually being restored to beauty.

A worship chorus that fits well with a restoration theme is "In His Time"—a Scripture, Isaiah 55. Suggested car activity: Brainstorm and list all the restoration words that begin with the prefix, RE (REbuild, REclaim, REnew—there're lots more). Use these words to praise Him for being your REsurrected REdeemer

Chapter Three/

I Am the King of Kings and Lord of Lords

"Almost as far back as I can remember, I talked to God," Lucinda said. "Telling God about my day as I played alone with my dolls outside under the big trees in our yard met a need in my life. I'd whisper everything outloud for Him to hear. As little as I was, I felt we had a special friendship that was more important than anything else in my life.

"But the day I most remember was the day I asked His Son to be Savior and Lord of my life. I was seventeen and the memory is as vivid now as then.

"It was an old church—not very big. And the man who spoke—I don't remember his name. But what he said—I'll never, never forget.

"He talked about the cross. For the first time in my life I saw Jesus dying on the cross for *me*. Really saw Him. I felt the emotion, the horror of that thick darkness.

"I pictured Jesus, blood dripping off His forehead from

that ugly thorn crown; the skin of His chest stretched tight over His bones. He looked at the crowd with love and compassion shining out of His eyes. In His ears He might still be hearing the words they shouted, 'Crucify Him! Crucify Him!'

"Yet He stood on that nail, gasping for breath, crying aloud, 'Father, forgive them, they know not what they do.'

"It did something to me inside. Jesus, my friend, the One I'd talked with as a little girl. He died for me. It was an awful death.

"All of a sudden I saw myself as He saw me, sinful, doing my own thing no matter who I hurt. Jesus' Father had to turn away from Him while He was on that cross. For the first time in eternity Jesus was walled off from His Father. It was my sin that did it."

Lucinda's voice lowered. "Jesus loves me. He died for me. Took all my sin on His own back so to speak, so I wouldn't have to be judged guilty before God.

"The pastor read Romans 12:1 in the King James—I have it memorized, 'I beseech you therefore, brethren, by the mercies of God, that ye present your bodies a living sacrifice, holy, acceptable unto God which is your reasonable service.' He said, 'Isn't it reasonable that this Jesus who died for you, is asking you to give yourself to Him?"

Lucinda shook her head. "It was so reasonable. So very right. I went home and knelt beside my bed. I gave Him my entire self in the best way I knew how—the sin—the uncertainties—everything I ever hoped to be. I've never been sorry."

King of Kings

Lucinda moved restlessly. "Oh, I didn't really understand all of what I was doing. I mean, I had no idea that in the weeks, months, and years ahead, that my Lord would continue to show me areas of my life that I hadn't committed to Him.

"I think it's sort of like selling a piece of property. I mean, you agree to sell it for a certain price and then all of a sudden you discover the trees on it are worth a lot of money. And you say, 'Oh, Lord. If I had known this was included....'

"Later you discover a stream and go through the same process again. Then you find a gold mine or an oil well. And so it goes, on and on, areas you didn't know were inside you.

"But He knew. Even that day I gave myself to Him, He knew what was inside me. In a way, making Him King of your whole life is a process. It's kind of like what Amy Carmichael said, 'There is always something more in your life He wants to mark with the cross.'

"I've experienced that, I think. Yet there was that moment of giving myself into His hand without reservation. More than anything I wanted Him to take charge of my life. And He has. Except sometimes I forget and try to do things my own way.

"But He always pulls me back. 'Lucinda,' He says, 'you belong to me. I am your King of kings. Worship me only.'"

Who Is This King of Glory?

The Magi from the East recognized that the One they sought was a king. "Where is he who has been born king of the Jews?" they asked. "We saw his star in the east and have come to worship him."

God honored the search of these wise men by allowing the star to lead them. And when the star stopped, they found Jesus, a small child with his mother.

These men's emotional response was one of intense joy (Matthew 2:10). They bowed down and worshiped Him, opened their gifts, presented Him with treasures of gold, incense, and myrrh.

We don't know how they found out about Jesus. Perhaps they'd heard Jewish exiles chant King David's song in Psalm 24:8-10.

Who is this King of glory?
The Lord strong and mighty,
the Lord mighty in battle.
Lift up your heads, O you gates;
lift them up, you ancient doors,
that the King of glory may come in.
Who is he, this King of glory?
The Lord Almighty—
he is the King of glory.

Thorns, a Staff and a Cloak

A king and yet—each aspect of His kingly authority was mocked at His own trial.

Instead of a crown of gold, a crown of tangled thorns pressed into His forehead.

Instead of a king's scepter, a staff was placed in His right hand.

Instead of a royal robe, an old purple military cloak swung from His shoulders.

But the placard written to proclaim him a criminal—instead proclaimed Him King.

Jesus was and is the King of the Jews, the King of glory, the King of kings. And because Jesus was and is all these things, He is also Lord of lords.

Who is this Lord of lords?

Adonai, as a name of God, is almost always possessive, recognizing ownership. Throughout the Old Testament those who know God as *Adonai* consider themselves His servant.

Jehovah is speaking to Abram (Genesis 15:1). "Do not be afraid, Abram. I am your shield, your very great reward."

Abram replies, "O *Adonai*, what can you give me since I remain childless....You have given me no children; so a servant in my household will be my heir."

Abram knows what it means to be a master. He has men under him who go when he says go, who stay when he says stay. When he addresses his God by the title Sovereign Lord, he acknowledges that Jehovah is his master and has the right to possess him completely.

In those days slaves stood in much closer relationship to masters than hired servants who came and went as they pleased. Slaves were part of the family and they could expect protections, love and help, even while the slave was in submission to and depended completely on his master. Therefore, Abram could tell God, his Master, the desire of his heart. He knew his Master would listen because He cared about every detail of his life.

Jehovah Adonai responded to Abram. He took him outside and had him look at the stars. "Your offspring will be as numerous as the stars—try to count them."

David also acknowledges God as his *Adonai*.

David himself is a king, appointed by God. But in II Samuel 7:18-29 he sits in humility and awe before God and worships. "Who am I, O *Adonai Jehovah*, and what is my family, that you have brought me this far?....What more can David say to you? For you know your servant, O Sovereign Lord."

Worship. From Abram. From David.

There is joy in living and serving beneath the protection of *Adonai*. Because He owns us, we can lay before Him the desires of our heart. We can even give to Him those deep inside longings we keep hidden from others.

The Heart of the Rock
Opening our hearts before the Lord can be an act of worship. Lucinda tells how she gave her Lord the desires of her heart.

"The desires deep inside my heart weren't bad desires," Lucinda said. "Some of them were extra special—I think God even planted them there. The problem was that I didn't trust Him enough to let go of them. I held them inside my heart, refusing to release them.

"Instead of being a blessing, they turned into a weighty thing. And all the time His voice kept whispering to my heart, 'Just give them to me, Lucinda.'

"There came a day when they grew heavy to me, too. I knew what I needed to do.

"I picked up my Bible, my notebook, and a pen and walked down to the creek. I sat down on top of the culvert that goes under the road. My feet dangled high over the water as I began to write.

"Tears mingled with words that only my Lord could see as I wrote them down. The desires of my heart were precious.

"Then I leaned over and tossed my tear streaked words into the water, watched the stream take the paper away. All of a sudden I couldn't bear it.

"I kicked off my tennis shoes and lowered myself into the dark culvert. Would my paper come out on the other side or would it be submerged in the dark tunnel?

"I felt like a small child as I splashed through the swiftly running water. But I had to know. I had to see.

"White flashed on the other side, then was gone, hidden beneath the water. I ran toward the spot. Stopped.

"The desires of my heart were inside an indentation in a rock. It was the only rock in the creek. And it was shaped like a heart.

"I turned away. I knew beyond all doubt that the most fragile part of me was safe with my Lord. He held them close to His heart. In the best way I knew how, I'd done my part. My desires were His responsibility now."

Lucinda had done what she needed to do. She gave the Lord of lords and King of kings the most precious thing she had. She gave Him the desires of her heart.

Worship, Our Most Valuable Service

As we offer to our Lord our sacrifice—our pain, our

joy, whatever is inside us—a wonderful thing happens. He draws near.

"The Lord your God is with you, he is mighty to save. He will take great delight in you, he will quiet you with his love, he will rejoice over you with singing" (Zephaniah 3:17).

Mary is a woman in whom the Lord delighted. She had spent time with Jesus and had rare insight in that she understood that her Lord would taste death for every man. In a sense, she was a support group of one because she understood His mission to earth. She knew He faced the cross.

Two days before the Passover we see her at the dinner at Simon's house. She slips in almost unnoticed as the men recline at the table. In her hand she clutches a jar of expensive perfume.

The house is filled with the odor as she breaks the jar and pours the perfume on her Lord's head and feet. That fragrant cloud, the aroma of the perfume she'd broken for His burial would linger with Him, follow Him to the Passover supper, the garden of Gethsemane, through the trials of the night. Unseen, its fragrance would permeate His darkness and assure Him of her love and support.

Supreme love and sacrifice are shown in this single act. Once Mary's jar was broken, she could never again hug it to herself. The contents could never be put back.

Jesus said, "She has done what she could. She poured perfume on my body beforehand to prepare for my burial. I tell you the truth, wherever the gospel is preached throughout the world, what she has done will also be told, in memory of her" (Mark 14:8-9).

Mary's life was a fragrance poured out. She gave her entire self to her Lord, her Master, her King. Her sacrifice was symbolized in the pouring out of her most valued possession—for Jesus. She gave her all to her Lord—with love. She worshiped at His feet.

What is worship? Worship is our response to God, showing

by our words and actions that He is worthy of our deepest love. When He shows us Himself on the cross, all we can do is bow before Him and whisper, "Thank you," then rise to give Him that part of ourselves we've been holding on to.

Helps in Setting the Sail:

1. Only as we surrender our lives to His Lordship are we able to influence others in that direction. Think about what it means to be under the authority of Jesus Christ. Read Romans 12:1-2 and paraphrase the words into a prayer that expresses your commitment.

2. Verbalizing your heart desires to your Lord and then releasing them to Him can be a step of growth. Ask God if this is something you need to do. If so, then do it.

3. A song or poem originating from your heart can be your special offering to the Lord. It's something no one but you can give. Write one that brings joy to your heart—because it gives joy to the heart of your God.

Suggestions for Family Sailing:

1. Provide each family member with a large paper heart. Encourage each one to write down the things they most desire, then share those desires with the Lord. You might even want to share your desires with one another. This can be a time of drawing closer to the Lord and one another.

2. Read Mary's story and talk about how her broken bottle represented her desire to worship Jesus. Uncap a bottle of perfume and splash each family member. Ask one another, "If your life could be spilled out as an offering to God, what kind of fragrance would you like it to be?" Give each person the opportunity to tell why they chose their particular fragrance.

3. Have a "Royal King" family night. Make a paper crown and allow each person to be in charge for 15 minutes to an hour. Afterward, talk about what it must have been like for Jesus, the King of kings and Lord of lords, to allow wicked

men to nail him to the cross. Discuss why He was willing to do this when all power and authority belonged to Him.

Close by reading Hebrews 1:8-9, 2:6-9; Revelation 11:15-18 aloud.

SECTION TWO/
HOW CAN I PREPARE MY HEART TO
WORSHIP YOU?

Chapter Four/
By Opening Your Heart To Me

Bryce walked into the Sunday School classroom. "I almost hate Sundays," he said. "Mark lost his Bible—we found it wedged between the washer and dryer.

"Mandy couldn't decide what dress to wear. Our tire went flat. And Julie and I had a fight in the car."

His gaze fastened on the blackboard. Someone had written, *If you call the Lord's holy day honorable and if you honor it by not going your own way and not doing as you please...then you will find your joy in the Lord.* "And rejoice before the Lord your God at the place he will choose as a dwelling for his Name—you, your sons and daughters" (Deuteronomy 16:11).

Bryce gestured at the words. "That's certainly not true in our family—at least not this morning."

A Prepared Heart

All of us can probably identify with Bryce's morning. Trouble and crisis come with living in a fallen world. It's the price we pay for being part of the human race...a fallen, sinful race.

No, we can't always keep track of important items or keep the car from going flat in the driveway. However, there are things we can do to make Sunday a day of worship and service. The parable of the sower and the seed Jesus told in Luke 8:5-15 helps us understand our responsibility.

The soil of Palestine was hard and dry and rocky. The farmers waited patiently for the autumn rains to soak and soften it before they began plowing. The ox-drawn plows they used were crude and, though covered with an iron sheath, it took hard labor to break up the soil.

Picture a farmer in Jesus' day.

A leather, grain-filled bag suspended by a shoulder strap slaps against his thigh as he strides across the prepared field throwing out seed. Grain drifts from the farmer's hand to the ground, tossing out gold glints in the sunshine.

Alongside the field are scattered rocks and a well-trodden path. Large black birds soar overhead. Some lower their wings and settle onto the ground beside the path, pecking at the fallen seeds.

In an agrarian society, Jesus used the most vivid picture He could, the seed and the soil, to uncover rich spiritual truth. "The seed," He told the disciples, "is the word of God." The disciple James heard His words that day on the mountainside. When he wrote his epistle the image was still vivid. He said, "...humbly accept the word planted in you..." (James 1:21).

God's Word planted in our hearts—the seed. Who can begin to understand or measure the wondrous fruit producing potential in a single seed?

The soil—the varied conditions which either promote or stifle spiritual fruit-bearing. What can we do to prepare the soil

46

of our hearts so that they produce a crop?

Break Up Your Hard Ground

The prophet Hosea gives a beautiful illustration. "Sow for yourself righteousness, reap the fruit of unfailing love, and break up your unplowed ground; for it is time to seek the Lord, until he comes and showers righteousness on you" (Hosea 10:12).

So did Isaiah. "For as the soil makes the sprout come up and a garden causes seeds to grow, so the Sovereign Lord will make righteousness and praise spring up before all nations" (Isaiah 61:11).

In Luke's parable (Luke 8), Jesus went on to explain that the path's hard soil represented those who hear God's Word, but the Word is snatched out of their hearts by the devil so that they won't believe and be saved.

The hard pathways were thoroughfares for travel. They illustrate distracted lives, intent on their own destinations, ideas, and purposes. Satan is quick to confuse those blinded by self-preoccupation. He easily distracts them so that God's Word isn't heard.

The seeds growing with the thorns did a little better than those on the rock and the hard path. They sprouted and grew. But because of the thistles, their growth was stifled. Instead of strong productive plants, they became stunted, bearing grain stalks that never became fully ripe.

The love of money, worries, pleasures, and selfishness are the thistles of life. They can prevent the seed of the Word from reaching full maturity in human hearts. So can the turmoil resulting from unfulfilled commitments and the bitter pain or guilt over unforgiven sin.

Distraught Sunday morning hassles sap us of vitality. They keep us from praising our Lord, from worshiping with our total concentration.

All these things keep us from producing the harvest of

47

faith—works for which the seed was sown.

But there is a good soil—a prepared soil—a soft soil. In this kind of soil the seed is able to put down deep roots.

This kind of soil doesn't just happen.

Preparing our hearts to worship God takes hard work, discipline, and perseverance.

Spring Rain and Pools of Water

The last soil in our parable is a picture of hearts who are willing to open themselves up to the life-giving water of the Word.

The Israelites in exile on their way home were a weakened people, desperately needing God's Word to revive their hearts. Isaiah brought them a message of hope from the Lord of lords and King of kings.

The poor and needy search for water, but there is none; their tongues are parched with thirst. But I the Lord will answer them; I, the God of Israel, will not forsake them. I will make rivers flow on barren heights, and springs within the valleys. I will turn the desert into pools of water, and the parched ground into springs. I will put in the desert the cedar and the acacia, the myrtle and the olive. I will set pines in the wasteland, the fir and the cypress together, so that people may see and know, may consider and understand, that the hand of the Lord has done this, that the Holy One of Israel has created it. (Isaiah 41:17-20)

These verses are for all of us with parched and thirsty hearts. Our God invites us to call on Him, to open ourselves up to His life-giving flow.

His promise: renewal—revival.

His desire: that we might proclaim His praise (Isaiah 43:20-21).

Developing a Personal Worship Time

No, worship doesn't just happen. We are responsible to cultivate our hearts during the week through personal application. That doesn't necessarily mean Bible study, although study may be part of it. Mostly it is loving interaction with the Lord through prayer and the Word.

I've talked with and discipled many people. One thing I've observed—those who worship during their personal quiet time are the servants. The fruit producers. They're the ones who come to church on Sunday morning in anticipation of meeting their Lord. They're learning how to open their hearts to receive what God has for them.

How *do* we open ourselves up to Him?

One way is to turn to the Psalms. Select one to put in your own words. Either rephrase the words into a prayer inside your heart, speak or sing them outloud, or write them down on paper.

Psalms Now by Leslie Brandt are examples of paraphrased Psalms written to help you respond to God. So is the Creation Praise Series by Ward Patterson (*Under His Wings, Out of His Heart, Into His Love*). But they can't take the place of the ones you rephrase to fit your need.

The prayers of other Bible characters show us even more about opening our hearts to God: Hannah, Solomon, Daniel, Zechariah, and Paul are only a few of those whose prayers are recorded for our instruction. Jeremiah is still another.

A Man With a Transparent Heart

Jeremiah is a prophet who lived a transparent life before others and before God. An intimate relationship with his Lord is what kept him persisting through forty years of ministry to a people who rejected him. Even when thrown into a cistern, he didn't defect. Later, bound with chains, led away from the city he loved more than he loved life itself, he persevered. He remained faithful to God even when outward appearances would seem to say God wasn't faithful to him.

A careful study of Jeremiah and Lamentations reveal the source of his strength.

Jeremiah prays.

Seven of his prayers are preserved for us in the book that bears his name. Not one of them can be described as particularly proper—they certainly aren't couched in lofty theological platitudes. Nor do they smack with half-truths.

Jeremiah's prayers are real, often agonizing; he's honest with God on an intimate level. He's learned to pour out his heart like water in the presence of his God.

Listen to his prayer in Jeremiah 15:15-18:

> *You understand, O Lord; remember me and care for me. Avenge me on my persecutors. You are long-suffering—do not take me away; think of how I suffer reproach for your sake. When your words came, I ate them; they were my joy and my heart's delight, for I bear your name, O Lord God Almighty. I never sat in the company of revelers, never made merry with them; I sat alone because your hand was on me and you had filled me with indignation. Why is my pain unending and my wound grievous and incurable? Will you be to me like a deceptive brook, like a spring that fails?*

What can we learn from his prayer?

Jeremiah addresses a personal God. He opens his heart, reveals what's going on deep inside. He shows us that prayer is intimate communication between two people who accept, respect, and love each other passionately, who are not afraid to take off their masks and reveal their hearts to one another.

Eugene H. Peterson in his excellent book about the prophet Jeremiah, *Run With the Horses*,[1] writes, "Prayer is...carefully protected and skillfully supported intimacy. Prayer is the desire to listen to God firsthand, to speak to God firsthand, then setting aside the time and making the arrangements to do it. It issues from the conviction that the living God is immensely important to me and that what goes on between us demands my exclusive attention." Jeremiah tells God exactly what he's experiencing inside. He prays his fear, confusion, and desperation. Eugene Peterson paraphrases verse 15 into these words, "God, you got me into this, now get me out!"[2] Jeremiah also prays his loneliness. "I sat alone because your hand was on me." He prays his hurt and doubts. "Why is my pain unending and my wound grievous and incurable?" His anger intrudes. "Will you be to me like a deceptive brook, like a spring that fails?"

Can you identify with the heartache behind his questions? God had revealed Himself to Jeremiah as the Fountain of Living Waters, and Jeremiah had faithfully preached that truth (Jeremiah 2:13). Now he's accusing God of being a "deceitful brook," one of those stream beds in the desert that looks as if water should be flowing in it, but when you arrive, all hopeful, tired, thirsty, you find it dry. Water only flows in it after a rain. It can't be depended upon between times.

Jeremiah's prayer is real. It expresses what's inside his heart—fear, loneliness, pain, doubt, anger.

We all experience these feelings. But the question Eugene Peterson raises in his book is one we each need to raise in our hearts: "Do we pray them?"

Listening to God
Jeremiah pours out his heart, now he listens. This is what the Lord says:

"If you repent, I will restore you that you may serve me; if you utter worthy, not worthless words, you will be my spokesman. Let this people turn to you, but you must not turn to them. I will make you a wall

51

to this people, a fortified wall of bronze; they will fight against you but will not overcome you, for I am with you, to rescue and save you," declares the Lord. (Jeremiah 15:19-21)

Over and over in his preaching, Jeremiah had urged his people to repent. Now God gives the same message back to Jeremiah.

God gives Jeremiah further instructions. He reaffirms His call to him, reassures him that He's with him.

Jeremiah's heart is open. He is able to experience the comfort of His God.

How does God respond to the pain in our hearts as we open ourselves to Him?

He pours His comfort in.

    Tears tumble from our heart
    Empty us of self
    Accentuate our humanity
    Refresh our spirits
    Splash into His heart

Jeremiah not only shows us his heart, he reveals to us the heart of God. An open heart is a prepared heart.

A prepared heart worships.

FOOTNOTES

[1]Taken from *Run With the Horses* by Eugene H. Peterson, © 1983 by InterVarsity Christian Fellowship of the USA. Used by permision of InterVarsity Press, P.O. Box 1400, Downers Grove, IL 50515.

[2]*Ibid.*

[3]*Making Sunday Special* by Karen Burton Mains, © 1987, Word Inc., Dallas, TX. Used with permission.

Helps in Setting the Sail:
1. Read and paraphrase a Bible prayer to help you express your heart to God. It may be a prayer when you're...
- longing for God (Psalm 42:1-2).
- disappointed in ministry (Jeremiah 15:15-18).
- filled with unanswered questions that demand an explanation (Psalm 77).
- asked to do a job and you're filled with feelings of inadequacy (Exodus 3).

2. Do a soil test on the hearts of the following Bible characters (1 is soft; 10 is rock hard):
A. Joanna (Luke 8:3) _____
B. John (Revelation 1:9) _____
C. Uzziah (II Chronicles 26:4-5,16) _____
D. Demas (II Timothy 4:10) _____
E. Elymas (Acts 13:6-10) _____

3. Use the following questions to evaluate the condition of your heart:
Do I anticipate Sunday? If not, why not?
How often do I cancel attractive weekend plans because I don't want myself or my family to miss Sunday worship? How often do I so eagerly look forward to worship that I'm at church 10-15 minutes early?
How many times am I stirred in my soul by the worship songs and/or the Scripture reading? When does church attendance become more than an activity? When does it begin to shake the very depths of my being?
How does the way I use my time reflect the importance or lack of importance God's Word has in my life? How is the condition of my heart soil being expressed in my life?

4. Do a soil test on your heart. Be honest. On a scale of one to ten, how do you rate?

Suggestions for Family Sailing:

1. Demonstrate the principle of the open heart with an object lesson. You'll need two jars, one with a lid. Pour water over both as you explain what you've learned about opening your heart to the Lord. Use language children can understand. What happens when you pour water over the sealed jar? The open jar?

2. Read the parable of the sower and the seed (Luke 8). Simulate the three kinds of soil in Jesus' story in three separate pots. Plant a sunflower seed in each one. They will be a continuing visual to reinforce the principle: The fruit in my life is dependent on the Spirit within, where God's seed has been planted. But the condition of the soil in my heart is my choice.

3. Encourage children to illustrate the parable with a drawing. A simple figure of a farmer with an outstretched arm, seeds drifting from hand to ground, a path alongside, rocks tumbled beside it, soaring birds overhead and on the ground behind the sower.

Add results: A bird with a seed in its beak, a withered sprout on hard ground with a burning sun overhead, thorns and an immature grain stalk side by side, a fully developed stalk of grain in the well-tilled field.

Display the picture as a reminder of the biblical principle in #2.

4. Read *Making Sunday Special* [3] by Karen Burton Mains. Make a list of suggestions tailored for your family from it and post them where you can read it often. Such as:

During the week:

1. Read the Word. Sit before your Lord (I Samuel 7:18). Ask Him to still your heart.

On Saturday:
1. Go to bed early so you'll be ready for church in the morning.
2. Solve the clothes hassle by deciding then what you will wear. And don't forget to locate shoes!
3. Pray:
   A. Spend time in confession so all will be right between yourself and the Lord when you worship.
   B. Ask the Lord to help you to be ready to receive the nuggets of truth He has specially designed for you during the Sunday service.
   C. Ask Christ to make you sensitive to the needs of people in the body. Ask Him to give you grace to give that smile, that hug, those words to minister comfort.

On Sunday:
1. Get up early enough so you won't feel rushed.
2. Program your morning so that you get to church early.

Chapter Five/
By Listening To Me

Two privates, George Elliott and Joseph Lockard, were manning a portable radar unit on Oahu Island in the Pacific Ocean on December 7, 1941.

At 6:45 a.m. they picked up a suspicious blip on the screen and reported it to Fort Shafter. The operator thanked them and recorded the report.

At 7:02 a.m. a large blip, the largest Elliott had ever seen, appeared on the oscilloscope. The blip looked like two waves of planes speeding straight for the Hawaiian Islands.

Even though Lockard said it wasn't necessary, Elliott called the information center. "There's a huge number of planes coming in from the north...."

Private Joseph McDonald, at the information center switchboard, replied that he would record the sighting. But nobody else was there, and he didn't know what he could do about it.

Later McDonald called the radar station back. Lockard answered the phone. By that time he was excited. The screen was filled with planes headed for Oahu. Lockard insisted on speaking with Lt. Kermit Tyler.

Tyler came to the phone. Lockard argued that he had never seen so many planes—92 miles away, coming in at 180 mph. Tyler listened, then said, "Well, don't worry about it." A short time later Lockard and Elliott closed down the radar set.

Around 8 a.m., 360 Japanese airplanes attacked Pearl Harbor. They sank four battleships and three destroyers, damaged many other ships, and killed 3,581 people.

Joseph McDonald and Kermit Tyler at the information center had all of the data they needed to alert the armed forces at Pearl Harbor of an oncoming attack.

But McDonald wasn't sure what to do with the information he received. Tyler didn't take it seriously.

Helps for Your Quiet Time

The Bible has all the information we need to enable us to worship God in Spirit and in truth. But we don't always know how to use it. We may not take it seriously enough to develop the spiritual discipline that enables us to respond to Him.

Someone has likened the spiritual dimension of our lives to a beautiful mosaic. Bible study, memorization, listening to the Word preached from the pulpit, prayer—these are all an important part of our mosaic.

But the background of our mosaic is our quiet time. Without this background—our quiet time with the Lord—our lines can become blurred, our beauty impaired. Bible study and listening to sermons can become simply a quest for knowledge, prayer and memorization a mere parroting of words.

It's when we begin to spend time alone with Him that we begin to catch glimpses of who He is—begin to see that knowing God is a process that will take us through life and through eternity. His majesty and glory are so great that we only catch glimpses while we're here on earth. Yet even these little glimpses overwhelm us. The more we recognize this, the more exciting this process of getting to know God becomes.

Keeping a notebook in your daily quiet time can be a tool through which you explore various techniques and get to know God better. It can help develop the discipline you need to keep you persevering in personal worship.

The notebook, often called a journal, is a daily log in which you record verses, insights, prayers, and personal applications. On its pages you can ask questions, sort through thoughts and perplexities. It can help you put Jesus Christ in the center of your problems and decision making.

After you read a psalm or another portion to help you open your heart, go to the book of the Bible you've chosen to read through. Start at the beginning and, each day, confine yourself to one portion that's a complete thought. Read it three times.

Although the quiet time isn't a time for study, I often use the Bible study technique of observation at this time. Listing my observations into my notebook helps me see more clearly what God is saying to me through His Word. It helps me formulate the key principle I've asked God to teach me that day.

What Is a Key Principle?

A principle is a timeless, unchanging truth stated with an action verb. This truth refers to who God is and what He wants to do in our lives. It tells what will happen to us as we respond to that truth—or refuse to respond to it.

A student in one of my classes on Bible study methods printed the word principle into her notebook. She transformed the tails of the p's into legs by adding feet. "This is to remind me that truth without action is useless." A principle helps us put action to our learning.

I learn to think God's thoughts as I read, observe, and pray. In dependence on the Holy Spirit, I can then turn what I've learned into a key principle that I can carry into my day.

For example, a key principle from my time in Philippians

4:4-9: "The peace of God guards the hearts and minds of those who pray." From this single principle I know that God stands guard over my peace when I commit my anxieties to Him.

Then comes application. How am I to integrate into my life the truth I just wrote down? What specific steps of action am I going to take?

The first step for me is to present my anxieties and cares to God. I do this by asking the Holy Spirit to bring to my mind those worries and problems that are robbing me of peace. Listing each one is a way of presenting them to God.

When I write a personalized prayer, God and I become partners in the practical working out of that truth.

"Lord, I want to rejoice in your peace today. But I find it hard because of the anxieties I'm facing. I give them to you now and praise you for the peace you've promised. I claim that peace in the name of Christ."

Biblical principles can be gleaned from any passage, Old and New Testament narratives, parables, the prophets.

A life-changing key principle from the eighth chapter of Nehemiah: "Joy awaits those who respond to God's written word." Another, this one a warning, from Isaiah 42:18-25: "God pours out His judgment on those who willfully refuse to obey His Word."

"Who Are You, Lord?"

Another important question you can ask God as you come to His Word is, "What truth about yourself do you want to communicate to me right now?"

"Who are you, Lord?" (Acts 22:8) was the first question Paul asked on the way to Damascus right after he saw the light on the road. When we come to the Word with this question in our hearts, we're going to worship. We're going to respond to Him.

Thursday, 2/26, Hebrews 2:1-4:
"Lord, who are you?"
"I am the One who keeps you from drifting away....Your Anchor, the Proclaimer of the message of salvation, Sovereign Lord, Distributor of the gifts of the Holy Spirit."
Application prayer: "Lord, your message is binding. Please, don't let me drift away. The salvation you've given me is precious, holy. I want to hold it in awe always. And if I hold it in awe, I won't ignore it."

"What Would You Have Me to Do?"
The second question Paul asked is, "What shall I do, Lord?" (Acts 22:10). In other words, "What truth do you want me to put into action today?"

Be alert for specifics—an attitude deep inside that He wants to deal with—a bitter root, resentment, a desire to be first. A person you've wronged whom you need to go to and ask for forgiveness.

He may bring to your mind someone's needs, use you to encourage that person with a phone call, a note, a visit. Provide a meal or a trip to town. Mow a lawn, fix a fence.

He may ask you to talk less and listen more. Or do just the opposite, to not be afraid to open your mouth when you have something to say.

Thursday, 2/26, Hebrews 2:1-4 (continued)
"Lord, what would you have me to do?
"The words, 'must,' 'careful,' 'ignore,' and 'proclaimer' grab me. I've listened. Now, Lord, help me to be very aware of what I'm to be—I, too, am to be a proclaimer of salvation—even to those I'm scheduled to meet with today. Open their hearts. Open my mouth."

Other Suggestions...
A group committed to discipling one another explored

different techniques in their quiet time. Paraphrasing verses into their own words became a favorite with several.

What is a paraphrase? Paraphrasing is simply putting God's Word into your own words so that it is personalized to your needs and situation.

Lisa's paraphrase of Psalm 42:1-2 became a prayer: "Lord Jesus, I long for you. But instead of being like a thirsty deer running to the water, I feel like an uprooted plant left laying on a cement path. I guess I need you to send someone along who'll pick me up instead of stepping on me. Someone who'll help me to you."

So did Ron's rendition of Ephesians 1:3: "I offer praise to you, Lord God, because of who you are; you are the Father of my Lord Jesus Christ. You've showered me with spiritual blessings from heaven. They rest on me because of my position in Jesus Christ. I am your son. I am chosen to sing Christ's praises."

Biblical truth can sometimes be illustrated with a simple picture. Nancy drew a tree filled with fruit of the Spirit as she read and meditated on Psalm 1. The roots of the tree she drew in her notebook went deep—deep—down, then reached out exploring tendrils to the river.

Jim's leering faces illustrating the lusts of the flesh in Colossians 3:5-9 were ugly enough to make anyone want to "put to death...whatever belongs to your earthly nature." Paula drew a stick figure and clothed it with the virtues listed in Colossians 3:12. She used a red pen to sketch a belt to represent love, to bind "...them all together in perfect unity" (3:14).

Taking a word, a theme, or a central message that the Holy Spirit illuminates in a particular portion of Scripture and creating an acrostic is a fun way to remember truth. They can stand alone or be combined with other thoughts.

Lucinda spent several months in the book of Hebrews. She

summarized the truth she'd learned about Jesus as her High
Priest by creating the following acrostic.

H oly	P recious
L I ght-giver	R ighteous
G lorious	I nterceder
H elper	R E deemer
	S ervant
	T HE LAMB OF GOD

Writing down a verse or phrase, followed with a personal
response placed inside parentheses, is another way you can
interact with the Lord. A sample from Kathy's notebook:
My soul followeth hard after Thee:
(Who else is there?)
Thy right hand upholdeth me.
(Strength)

Those Who Don't Quit
A personal quiet time can be a tool in the hand of Almighty
God to cultivate a believer's Christ-likeness.

In the parable of the sower, the seeds planted in the good soil
put down roots that enabled them to persevere and produce a
crop. They were those who clung to Christ's teaching, no
matter what it cost, who didn't quit.

The disciples' hearts were cultivated fields. They knew
what it meant to leave all behind in order to be with their
Master. They kept on following and praying and worshiping
even when they didn't understand.

It's interesting that this parable is preceded by the specific
mention of three women—Mary Magdalene, Joanna, the wife
of an important Herodian official—and Susanna.

Jesus had cast seven devils from Mary Magdalene. She
had been freed to serve—and serve Him she did; no
family, no home, Mary Magdalene was with Him and

the disciples wherever they went.

Joanna had left the comfortable court life to follow Jesus across the countryside. Her commitment to Him was such that she'd even given money from her own pocket to finance His ministry. She had, along with Mary Magdalene and Susanna, taken part in the cooking and sewing.

These women's hearts were like plowed fields, their lips expressed their adoration, their hands their love and service. What reassurance this parable must have held for them and the disciples! They had chosen to be in the presence of their Master. They were the called, the ones who endured and served, who continued. They were the ones who bore fruit.

John was one of these disciples. A simple, ordinary fisherman, John left all to follow Jesus. He was with Jesus when He spoke with the woman at the well. He saw Him heal the blind, the crippled, the lepers. Gradually, he grew into close companionship with Jesus; he was with Him when God revealed His glory in Jesus' transfiguration on the mountain.

In the Gospel which he wrote, John refers to himself at the last supper as, "One of them, the disciple whom Jesus loved, was reclining next to him" (John 13:24). Propped up on his elbow, his feet extended away from the table, John leaned his head against Jesus' chest. The Heartbeat of heaven filling his head, his heart. There at that memorable supper, he held a privileged place of nearness.

John had an intimate relationship with Jesus. He spent prime time with his Lord.

It is significant that this man, near the end of his life, was chosen to look into heaven and write what he saw. He also wrote what he heard—the glorious praise songs the elders sang around the throne.

Spending time in God's presence does for us what it did for the women, the disciples, and John. It makes us vulnerable to the Holy Spirit and prepares our hearts to enter His courts with praise.

A personal quiet time can be a time of personal worship with our Savior, the Creator, the Lord of lords and King of kings.

Helps in Setting the Sail:
Our Lord has given us everything we need to live a life of godliness (II Peter 1:8). We only need to set the sail...and keep sailing.

1. Spend time listening to God this week. Select a portion of Scripture that's a complete thought and read it three times. List your observations. Practice writing a key principle and an application prayer from one or more of them. Remember, a principle is an unchangeable truth that is applicable to your life today.

2. Read Acts 22:3-21. Write the two questions Paul asked God into your notebook or on a sheet of paper. Use them to draw you into a deeper understanding of who God is and what He wants to do in your life.

3. Commit yourself to a week with the Gospel of Mark. The first chapter is divided into seven complete thoughts in the *NIV Study Bible*. Use the "Who are You, Lord?" / "What would you have me to do?" technique.

4. Do one of the other suggestions—an acrostic, paraphrase, a verse response or an illustration. Share it with your family or another person.

Suggestions for Family Sailing:
1. Children can be taught to ask the same questions Paul asked. Encourage them to read Acts 22:3-21 and underline Paul's questions. Explain that they can ask God those same questions as they read other Scripture passages.

Direct them to portions that teach easily grasped spiritual truth about who God is. For instance: *Rock* (Deuteronomy 32:4, II Samuel 22:2-3, Psalm 61:1-3, 92:12,14-15, Isaiah

26:4); *Shepherd* (Psalm 23:1, John 10:11-14, Hebrews 13:20-21, I Peter 5:4, Revelation 7:17); *Lamb of God* (John 1:29, Acts 8:32, Revelation 5:6-12); *Savior* (I Chronicles 16:35, Psalm 79:9, Luke 2:11, I John 4:14-15); *Bright and Morning Star* (II Peter 1:19, Revelation 2:28, 22:16); *Light of the World* (Micah 7:8, Matthew 17:2, John 8:12, Revelation 21:23).

2. Use one of the following suggestions for a special family night.

A. Conduct a "Who are you, Lord?" family gathering. Give each child and adult a file card with Scriptures that teach a truth about God (Scripture suggestions in #1). Each person shares what they found out about God from their verses.

Use those truths to create an original song. Each person writes a sentence of praise to God for the attribute or truth about God they discover. Everyone helps organize the sentences into a family praise song.

Additional Suggestion: Draw pictures to illustrate the completed family praise note. Send a copy to grandparents or to other special family friends.

B. Conduct an "A Proverb Photo" family night. Write several Proverbs on separate sheets of paper. (Chapters 10–30 are filled with many picturesque and fun Proverbs.) Give one to each family member to illustrate.

Ask, "What does this teach you about what God does or doesn't like?"

Be prepared for some good laughs over the completed "photos."

Chapter Six/
By Talking To Me

Continuing with our Lord means continuing to worship.
Continuing to worship means continuing in prayer.
   Is prayer really essential for worship?
   Yes!
   If so, why is it so difficult to pray before we worship...while
we worship?
   How do we pray for our pastor? Our church?
   One of the most memorable tongue lashings I ever received
was delivered by a deacon following a Sunday morning
worship service; I had just preached.
   He thumped the face of his wristwatch with his fingertips as
he told me the sermon was too long. The content all wrong.
   All the time he talked my thoughts raced.
   *If the sermon was so bad, why weren't you praying for
me?*
   *Did you notice the man in front of you? He doesn't know our
Lord. He leaned forward as he listened, and I saw hunger in
his eyes. Were you praying for his salvation?*

And the woman at the end of your pew. Her son's in jail and she's hurting....

Pray As You Worship

When I look at the people gathered to worship and see a head bowed here, another there, I feel a sense of expectation. God has always promised to meet with those who seek Him.

Picture the Holy Spirit—a restless wind—stealing unseen and often unperceived into churches around the world. He whispers. He sings. He touches a heart here, another there, almost with exploring fingertips. If a wall is erected around that heart, that body of believers, He grieves. He can do no great work there.

Herbert Lockyer in *All the Divine Names and Titles in the Bible* [1]writes of Him:

He can search – and what a Searcher! (I Corinthians 2:10).

He can speak – and what a voice! (Acts 8:29, I Timothy 4:1, Revelation 2:7).

He can testify – of God, of Christ, and of truth (John 14:26,27).

He can teach – and who teaches like Him? (John 14:26, 16:12-14, Nehemiah 9:20).

He can lead – and always the right way (Romans 8:14).

He can command – and blesses obedience (Acts 16:6-7).

He inspires Scripture – and speaks only through it (John 16:13, II Peter 1:21).

The Holy Spirit is the mighty wind of God. His voice can and will be heard if we will but spread wide the sails of our heart.

As we give ourselves to Him in adoration and praise, an invitation is written on the sail, "Work in me, Holy Spirit, I need you. I want you."

A prepared heart participates in the worship service.

Continue in Prayer

Silent prayer should be a part of every individual's service. Believers become active participants as they pray for the service, the worship leaders, the pastor as he preaches. It's a ministry in which every person in the body of Christ can take part.

What else can we pray for?

We can pray for our church as a body.

A pastor friend said God was leading him to pray, for his own church, the various prayers Paul prayed. "I'd been praying for the various individuals when suddenly it hit me, I need to pray for the church as a body." He smiled. "Certainly I need to talk to God about the elbows—and the tongues. But I also need to pray for the whole body."

He paraphrased Colossians 1:9-11. "I haven't stopped praying for South Hills Baptist. I keep asking God to fill it with the knowledge of His will through all spiritual wisdom and understanding. I pray this so that as a body they will bear fruit in every good work, growing in the knowledge of God, being strengthened with all power according to his glorious might so that they may have great endurance and patience...."

We can pray for the people who have an active part in the behind-the-scenes ministries. Those who teach Sunday School...who care for babies and toddlers. Those who type bulletins and fix doors and clean restrooms.

It takes a lot of hands to keep our churches functioning. So many may come to our mind that we may feel overwhelmed. If that happens, we can ask God, "who do you want me to pray for right now?" Allow His Spirit to bring faces and names, specific jobs or needs to your mind.

We can pray for the people in the worship service. Are there unsaved people present? Those who are hurting? Who are needy?

Involvement in people's lives during the week sensitizes us to the needs of those around us. A husband and wife sit side by side. But a rebellious son has stretched tension between them. These parents aren't working together anymore. They're no longer trying to communicate.

A man sits with shoulders slumped. He's being sued by a man he thought was his best friend.

A teenager stands by the door, alone. Running away from home doesn't seem like a bad idea—at least not right now.

Allowing the Spirit to interact with our spirit means we pray. It might mean involvement. An arm around a shoulder, an invitation to lunch. It could mean asking that one, "How can I pray for you this week?" or "What can I do?" It might mean asking God to give you creative ideas as to how you might help meet needs so painful they can't be expressed.

Prayer and participation on Sunday morning results as an overflow of the Holy Spirit and the Word working together. It comes when the Word is given freedom to interact with the will.

It's part of setting the sail.

Praying With One Another

Another way to set the sail is by praying with other believers during the week. Jesus' disciple seemed to understand this when he said, "Lord, teach us to pray" (Luke 11:1).

The prayer Jesus shared with them has a pattern that has instructed believers through the ages.

A group of believers gather in a circle, their Bibles open to Matthew 6:9-13:

"This is how you should pray:

"'Our Father in heaven, hallowed be your name, your kingdom come, your will be done on earth as it is in heaven. Give us today our daily bread. Forgive us our debts, as we also have forgiven our debtors. And lead us not into temptation, but deliver us from the evil one.'"

Heads bowed, eyes open, Bob and Lisa, Travis and Sandy are learning that bringing God's Word into their prayers helps them pray in ways that lead them beyond their human understanding.

"Our Father—" Bob hesitated, unsure. "Lord, that means you're my father. And children talk to their fathers."

Sandy continued Bob's thought. "Father, my Father. You are in heaven. You're even higher than the heavens. There isn't anything on earth that's too big for you. You have authority over all nations—"

"and presidents—" Bob added.

"Churches, too," Lisa said. "Lord, you're our head."

Bob and Sandy joined in. "Your name is holy."

"You are purity. And beauty."

"Lord, I need you."

"I need you, too," Bob confessed. "Except seeing you as holy and pure and higher than anything or anybody makes me see my sin. Lord, forgive me. My attitude toward my brother is rotten. My thoughts went round and round last night. I wanted revenge. Please, Father, cleanse my mind. My heart."

Travis prayed aloud for the first time. "Lord, that's your will for us on earth, isn't it? A cleansed heart. Lord, I pray for Bob. That he'll be able to put aside his sinful thoughts. That he'll choose to pray for his brother, not hate him."

"Lord, give Bob the grace he needs to forgive," Lisa whispered.

Sandy reached out and took Lisa's hand. "Give us today what we need in the area of our physical needs. Lisa's mother needs a place to stay—Lisa can't take care of her any more. Please help them find a good nursing home. One that can give her mother the loving daily care she needs."

"Our church has needs, too," Travis said. "We barely have enough to pay salaries—and we're behind in mission giving. Lord, press our hearts to give—just a little bit more."

"And forgive us," Lisa prayed, "for being self-centered

instead of people-centered."

"Lord, I'm being tempted right now to think mostly of me. I'd much rather go to the coast this weekend, but I've been away several Sundays. I need to be in your house. I need to worship you."

"Our church needs Bob, Lord," Travis said. "We need him here with us, worshiping, praying....We need his support."

"Pastor Norm needs his support, too," Lisa said softly. "And we need Norm's. We need to hear what you have to say to us through his message. Empty him of self, fill his mind with your Words. Give him words that will sing with your presence."

"Let him know we love him," Sandy said.

Bob put his finger on the last verse of the prayer. "Lord, you are the Mighty Deliverer. Protect Pastor Norm's family. His marriage. Lead him by delivering him from evil. Amen."

Heads lifted. Hands clasped.

Friends—more than friends. Their hearts are bonded together as God's Word and will was intertwined into their lives. They're a team, worshiping together. They're being prepared for Sunday.

What Happens When People Pray?

When I'm with God's people and hear them verbalize to God their concerns and hurts, their involvement in one another's lives, I'm stimulated. When I hear them pray for the ministry of the church, I'm encouraged. When they pray for me and the message I'm preparing, I'm energized.

Prayer shapes a sermon, transforming it into a message from God's heart. The Holy Spirit interacts with the minister's spirit and the daily experiences of his life. The sermon spread over his desk is transformed into a message from the Lord.

It happens because we have a God who is intimately linked to the hearts of His people, the hearts of those to whom He's given the responsibility to proclaim His words.

It happens when people pray both individually and together.

Wonder of the Church

There is a choreography that sailboats perform together on the water. It may be two boats, or four, or twenty-four. With unfurled sails, they skim the water, tacking right—then left—then right again. The turns are unexpected, sharp and beautiful. They move in unison, the wind behind them. A blue sail, a white one, a rainbow stripe. The sails catch sunshine first on one side, then the other. The water reflects sky and ripples the sails back to them. It slaps the sides of the boat, and the wind sings through the rigging. It is the dance of the sailboats, the song of the wind.

Just as there are certain things sailboats only do in company with other sailboats, there are some things we only experience as we pray and worship with other believers.

As we give ourselves to God in worship within the church setting, we share His beauty and His song with others. We are one in the Spirit; we are one with our Lord. Our worship is a beautiful song, a celebration that never grows old.

How good and pleasant it is when brothers live together in unity! It is like precious oil poured on the head...running down on Aaron's beard, down upon the collar of his robes. It is as if the dew of Hermon were falling on Mount Zion. For there the Lord bestows his blessing, even life forevermore (Psalm 133).

Harmony and love between brothers sanctifies God's people. We have been set apart to worship. We do it with our brothers and sisters.

As we yield to the oil of the Spirit, we give the Wind of God the freedom to do as He wills, to show us new aspects of who

He is and what He wants to do in our lives, both individually and as a body. We're renewed in ways we can never experience in private worship alone.

No, things may not go the way we want them to on Sunday morning. They may not go the way our pastor wants them to go either. But they can go God's direction when pastor and people participate as partners with God, worshiping and glorifying Him together.

FOOTNOTE

[1]Taken from the book *All the Divine Names and Titles in the Bible* by Herbert Lockyer. Copyright © 1975 by The Zondervan Corp. Used by permission.

Helps in Setting the Sail:
1. One of the greatest ministries we can participate in is praying for those actively involved in the worship service on Sunday morning. Copy the following onto a piece of paper and slip it into your Bible. Use it to guide you in silent prayer as you enter your church on Sunday morning.
What can I pray for as I worship?
My own heart
My church, other church bodies gathering around the world
My pastor, other pastors preaching the Word
Unseen people ministering out of public view
Others present in the service

2. Begin to personalize God's Word as you worship.
A verse to pray during the prelude: "You heavens above, rain down righteousness; let the clouds shower it down. Let the earth open wide, let salvation spring up" (Isaiah 45:8).
A verse to claim: "The poor and needy search for water, but there is none; their tongues are parched with thirst. But I the Lord will answer them" (Isaiah 41:17).

Suggestions for Family Sailing:
1. Children feel more at ease participating in prayer when the art of conversational prayer is practiced at home. Some children need additional encouragement. Introduce a subject, then ask each person to pray only one sentence regarding it.
Alternative suggestion: Pass out file cards on which you've written a single request. Each person writes a sentence prayer responding to that need.

2. Pray aloud for "our pastor, our deacons, Johnny's Sunday School teacher." Pray for specific needs you know your

75

church has. "Strength for Mrs. Hummel as she cares for the babies in the nursery; wisdom for the deacons as they decide on a plan to encourage church growth." This kind of prayer helps children develop a sense of belonging, encourages them to be pray-ers instead of criticizers.

SECTION THREE/
HOW SHOULD I ENTER YOUR PRESENCE?

Chapter Seven/
With Reverence

A teacher of teens asked her students what they thought the phrase, "The fear of the Lord" meant.

Brian shook his head. "I think it's being sort of scared. Not like God's your best friend at all. Instead He's far away—up there in the sky, white beard, big eye. When you do something wrong your stomach knots up—really tight."

"Reverence," Noelle said softly. "The fear of the Lord means reverence. Thinking about how great God is makes me want to be still. I think it's why I talk soft when I pray outloud."

Noelle, young as she was, recognized a quality in God that stilled her soul. His greatness created in her a holy awe that caused her spirit to bow before Him. She worshiped Him.

Silence, a Missing Ingredient

Stillness and silence is lacking in today's culture of activity and loud music. There is little opportunity to practice the discipline of silence and meditation, even in the context of the church.

Richard Foster, author of *Celebration of Discipline*, writes, "In contemporary society our Adversary majors in three things: noise, hurry, and crowds....If we hope to move beyond the superficialities of our culture, we must be willing to go down into the retreating silences...."

Dr. Edward L. Hayes, Executive Director of Mount Hermon Christian Conference Center in California, says, "Silence sets the stage for serious encounters with God...."

Yes, we're created to sing for joy and shout aloud to our Lord. We are invited to bring him an offering of thanksgiving and extol him with music and song. When we do these things, we acknowledge His greatness, His authority as King. "In his hand are the depths of the earth, and the mountain peaks belong to him" (Psalm 95:4).

This truth brings us into the silence where we experience the tender touches of our holy Father. "Come, let us bow down in worship, let us kneel before the Lord our Maker; for he is our God and we are the people of his pasture, the flock under his care" (Psalm 95:6-7).

But where is our Sunday morning silence? Children run up the aisle. People chat with one another as they find a place to sit. Some aren't aware that the organist is playing the prelude. Others don't know what a prelude is.

Do we fail in this area because we don't understand the meaning of the fear of the Lord?

What Is the Fear of the Lord?

The *NIV Study Bible* describes the "fear of the Lord" as "loving reverence for God that includes submission to his lordship and the commands of his word."

The fear of the Lord is the theme that ties together the varied segments of the book of Proverbs. It is to be sought after as the beginning point of knowledge and wisdom.

The words honor, revere, and reverence can help us further

understand the fear of the Lord. Respect is a common denominator in each of these words. Let's look at how *Webster's New World Dictionary* defines them.

Honor—high regard or great respect given, received, or enjoyed; especially glory; fame; renown; 2. a keen sense of right and wrong; adherence to action or principles considered right; integrity.

Revere—to regard with deep respect, love, and awe; venerate. SYN—revere implies a regarding with great respect, affection, honor, deference. Venerate implies a regarding as sacred or holy.

Reverence—1. a feeling or attitude of deep respect, love, and awe, as for something sacred. 2. a manifestation of this.

A young woman struggling in her marriage, sought counsel from an older woman.

"Do you respect him?" the older woman asked.

The younger one nodded slowly, thoughtfully.

"How do you respond to someone you respect?"

The younger one cupped her chin in her hands. "When I respect someone, I want to know their opinion. I ask questions, listen to what they have to say. I mull their words over in my mind."

Her blue eyes filled with emotion. "Most of all I just want to know them," she whispered. "Know what they think, how they feel. I want to look into their eyes."

Respect in human relationships comes as we spend time getting to know each other. Respect for God deepens as we spend time getting to know Him. As we worship.

"Real worship is intense," Ray Ortlund said at a seminar. "Therefore learn to worship Him with your emotions. Look into His eyes."

Seeing who Jesus is brings us to our knees in reverent submission. We're ready to respond, to listen. We want to know Him better. "Oh, that I might know Him and the power of His resurrection" becomes our heart cry.

Two Boats, Two Storms, One God

The fear of the Lord was stimulated in the disciples when, tossed with fear, buffeted by winds, they recognized the power of their almighty God.

A great storm, a great fear, and Jesus, walking on the water. "If it's you, bid me to come to you on the water," Peter cries. He steps onto the water, walks awhile, then...looks at the waves crashing around him. He begins to sink.

And Jesus stretches out His hand, returning with him to the boat. Immediately there is a great calm.

And Peter worships (Matthew 14:22-33).

Another storm, another boat, the same disciples. This time Jesus is with them, asleep on a pillow. The boat tips crazily. Waves threaten to swamp them.

"Save us, Lord!" the disciples cry.

Jesus gets up and rebukes the wind. Immediately, there is a great calm.

Awe fills the disciples' hearts, overflows in their words. "Who is this?" they wonder. "Even the wind and waves obey Him" (Mark 4:35-41).

Seeing His power and majesty kindles a desire deep within their hearts. They want to know Him better.

We respond by wanting to know Him better when we glimpse His power, too. We reverently worship when we recognize how much He wants to be involved in our lives.

But sometimes on Sunday morning, we're rather like the disciples being tossed by the storms. We're struggling, overcome by our own problems. No matter how we try, we can't get past them. Our thoughts bunch up and attack. Fear controls us.

When we cry out to Him—turn them over to Jesus—He settles and calms us. We see Him as the Almighty One with authority over all creation. And we are part of His creation.

We long to know Him for it is in knowing Him that we are enabled to worship Him in awe and wonder.

Get Ready

Karen Burton Mains in her book, *Making Sunday Special*,[1] writes, "John the Baptist shattered the wilderness of Judea with a loud shout. It was an ancient prophetic cry that had sounded repetitively from the mouths of God's faithful servants, 'Get ready! Get ready for the coming of the Lord!' For centuries holy men and women had stood in the wilderness of their own time and culture and shouted in one way or another so that others could hear, 'Get ready! The day of the Lord is at hand!'"

The prelude helps us get ready. It prepares our minds, hearts and emotions to recognize God's voice speaking to us.

Preparation, even for the Sunday morning prelude, begins during the week as we worship Him in our quiet time. It continues through the day as we take biblical principles and phrases with us and meditate on how He wants to weave them into our lives.

Geri leaned her elbows on the table. "You talk about meditating," she said earnestly, "but you know something? I've heard about meditation all my life—but I don't think I know how."

"Meditation is consciously thinking through a single key principle or a phrase or two from a verse," I explained. "You come at it from different angles. Personalize it through prayer."

I opened my Bible. "This morning I read Matthew 11:25-30 in my quiet time. All day my thoughts kept returning to Jesus' words, 'I will give you rest.'

"I ask questions. Since He's inviting me to rest, what's keeping me from resting? I'm tired. Am I exerting more effort than I should on concerns?

"Why am I gripping my burdens so tightly? Preoccupied with them, instead of Him? I need to let go my tight grip. I need to rest.

"I think back over the verse. 'Come to me, all you who are weary and burdened, and I will give you rest. Take my yoke

83

upon you and learn from me.' I realize He's saying that to me. He's the Inviter. I'm the weary one. He's asking me to come. To be yoked with Him. To learn from Him.

"I remember a boat I saw on the water, just resting. It has to rest in order to be prepared for sailing. If it's not prepared, it can't run with the wind.

"Rest means getting prepared for action.

"I pray, 'Lord, I come to you. Until I rest I can't be prepared by your Spirit to work side by side with you. In the best way I know how, I give you my burdens.'"

I closed my Bible. "I'm ready now to sit silently before my Lord with a spirit of expectancy when Sunday comes. I'm ready for my epiphany."

What Is Epiphany?

Epiphany simply means Christ's coming, usually celebrated at Christmas time. Christ's coming is looked forward to with anticipation.

As believers we can come every Sunday in expectation of meeting Him. Our meditation prepares us for that joyous moment when we discover God's personalized message for us during some point in the service.

It can happen during the prelude. A message may jump off the pages of our Bible as we meditate and the organ plays. As we think and rethink in an attitude of prayer and waiting, we're further prepared to hear His voice.

Later a song from the choir, the special music, or our own congregational singing may speak to deep places inside us. So can the words of a congregational prayer, a responsive reading. Or something in the sermon grabs our hearts.

So often we miss Christ's voice because our thoughts aren't captive to our heavenly Father. Instead of Him we think about whether or not we should fry our oysters in butter. We replay the game we saw last night in our mind. Or worry over something our spouse said.

But when He comes?

He illuminates our hearts to receive the truth He's specifically designed to minister to us in our area of need. He reveals Himself in ways that reach right down into our hearts and minds and shake us up.

A recognition of His person dawns on our senses. "You are glorious! Glorious! I adore you."

He comes! And He is beautiful.

Mary's Song

Mary Magdalene spoke words that have the power to make the senses sing. "I have seen the Lord!" It was the message Jesus gave her to give to the disciples...including Peter. It was the message of the empty tomb.

Did her heart form new words to the psalms the Israelites sang in their worship at the temple? Did she sing them aloud as she ran through the garden that long-ago Sunday morning?

Did the leaves of the olive trees whisper, "He is risen! He is risen!"? The splintering sunlight echo an affirmation?

"Ascribe to the Lord, O mighty ones,
ascribe to the Lord glory and strength.
Ascribe to the Lord the glory due his name;
worship the Lord in the splendor of his holiness."

"Let the sea resound, and all that is in it; let the fields
be jubilant, and everything in them! Then the trees of the
forest will sing, they will sing for joy before the Lord."

Mary had been present at Calvary. She experienced the darkness, felt the earthquake. She witnessed her Lord's dying glory. Perhaps her heart rang with words like...

"The voice of my Savior and the voice of my Father are
  One.
The voice of the Lord is over the garden.
The God of glory thunders;
  the Lord thunders over Mount Calvary.

The voice of the Lord is powerful;
the voice of the Lord breaks the olive trees.
The Lord breaks in pieces the chains of death.
He makes the hills around Jerusalem skip like calves
and Mount Calvary like a young wild ox.
The voice of the Lord strikes with flashes of lightning.
The voice of the Lord shakes Jerusalem.
The Lord shakes the gates of the city.
The voice of the Lord twists the oaks,
and strips the forests bare.
The voice of the Lord speaks my name."

"O Lord my God, I called to you for help,
and you came.
You healed my broken heart;
you made me sing."

Mary's feet must have skipped as she ran to tell the others, exultation bursting from her.

"You brought Jesus up from the grave.
You spared me from going down into the pit.
You went there so I wouldn't have to!"

"Sing to the Lord, O brethren of His;
praise his holy name.
For the Father's anger lasts only a moment
—that moment as darkness fell.
But His favor lasts a lifetime;
Weeping remains for a night,
Rejoicing comes in the dawn."

She stops in the middle of the path and spreads her arms wide. The sun falls on her face as she continues her song.

"At sunrise you came to me!
You turned my wailing into dancing;

You removed my sackcloth and clothed me with joy,
 that my heart may sing to you and not be silent.
O Lord my God, I will give you thanks forever."
*(Paraphrase taken from Psalm 29:1-9; I Chronicles
16:32-33; Psalm 30:2-5,11-12)*

Our own hearts can sing the message of the songs the Israelites sang as they worshiped. "I have seen the Lord."

These songs are our songs. Songs of reverence and anticipation, joy and submission. Songs that reflect a holy fear of the Lord.

FOOTNOTE
 [1]*Making Sunday Special* by Karen Burton Mains, © 1987, Word Inc., Dallas, TX. Used with permission.

Helps in Setting the Sail:

Prepare your heart for meeting Christ next Sunday by doing one or more of the following.

1. Choose a portion of Scripture that extols God's greatness and read it before you come to church and the worship service. Read it again as you listen to the prelude. Ask God to still your heart and prepare you to hear His voice.

Suggested Scripture: Psalm 95:1-7,17-18, 95:1-7, 103:8-14, 104:1,5-9,24-25,31-34, 116:1-9, I Chronicles 29:10-13.

2. Practice the art of meditating during the week. Slowly read and reread several verses. Pray, ask questions, consciously think and rethink Bible phrases and thoughts. Allow the Holy Spirit to shape them to your heart as you walk through each day.

3. Mary's song is a selection of verses that are descriptive of the joy she may have felt as she ran to tell the disciples the good news. Choose verses and phrases to match a song in your own heart. Or—select verses and phrases that express a song you wish you had in your heart. Either way, read, sing, or write the words down. Read or sing them back to your Lord.

4. You can ask God the same two questions Paul asked on the road to Damascus. The ones you learned earlier to ask in your daily quiet time, ask as you come to worship.

"Lord, who are you? What truth about yourself are you wanting to imprint on my life as I worship you this morning?

"Lord, what would you have me to do? How do you want me to live out the truth you're teaching me this hour? How am I to live it out this day? This week?"

Suggestions for Family Sailing:
Help your family prepare to meet the Lord on Sunday morning.
1. Print the words "GET READY!" in big bright letters on two sheets of paper. Put one on the refrigerator door, the other on the bathroom mirror. Use them as conversation starters to share what you've learned about how to get ready to hear Christ speak to you.

2. The spring season and the world of awakening blossoms can create a singing in the heart that can be likened to the joy we feel when a truth about who Christ is explodes inside us. Bring some blossoming flowers or branches into the house. Place them in water and call the family's attention to the gradual opening and the brilliant color. Ask how knowing Christ colors your lives. Use them to talk about preparing for Christ's coming and the joy that bursts inside us when we recognize new truth about who He is and what He wants to do in our lives.

3. Give each child a piece of paper on which you've written several Bible references. (You may choose appropriate verses from suggestion #1 in *Helps in Setting the Sail.*) Encourage them to tuck them inside their Bibles and read them during the prelude. Encourage them to write a prayer response.

4. Write down the two questions in #4 of *Helps in Setting the Sail* for each family member before you go to church. Give everyone opportunity to share what they wrote on their paper when you return home.
Additional sharing suggestion: Ask family members to share how and where they found their Lord speaking to them during the service.

Chapter Eight/
With Words of Praise

The universe is silent, dark. No wind... no waves pounding on the shore. No moon tilting in the heavens... no forest. And then...

Out of the silence comes a song.

A star burns in the vastness of space. Jesus Christ, present at creation. Jesus Christ, the Bright and Morning Star.

"Who laid its cornerstone—while the morning stars sang together and all the angels shouted for joy" (Job 38:6-7). Christ, the great director of this majestic choir, led a song that had never been sung.

Another night, another song. A star heralds the birth of the Savior of the world and angels burst into song. "Glory to God in the highest" reverberates across the centuries.

A new dawn. A new song.

Wonder fills our heart. We respond in worship.

What Is Worship?

The following sentences gleaned from Warren Wiersbe's book, *Real Worship*,[1] are worthy of consideration as we strive to answer this question.

"Worship is not an option, it is an obligation.

"Worship is not a luxury, it is a necessity.

"Worship is the response of all that man is to all that God is and does.

"Worship is the submission of all our nature to God.

"Worship is the highest and holiest experience of the Christian believer."

Worship is everything in us, responding to everything in Him. It expresses the worthiness of God back to Him.

Worship is the celebration of God. Praise is part of it.

Music—A Gift from the Heart of God

God is so wonderful in who He is, what He says, and what He does that the true wonder of worship is beyond us (Job 36:26, Job 11:7, Romans 11:33). How can a God who needs nothing desire words of praise from His creation?

I don't know—but He does. Over and over in the Psalms we're commanded to, "Praise the name of the Lord." Again and again the phrase, "the name of the Lord," surfaces. We find it three times in the first three verses of Psalm 113.

The name of the Lord summarizes in one glorious statement everything God is. He is worthy of our praise. "Holy, holy, holy is the Lord Almighty; the whole earth is full of his glory (Isaiah 6:3).

Psalm 113 enhances the song. The incomparable God enthroned on high stoops down to look at the heavens...stoops to look at the earth. He sees the poor crouched in the dust, the needy on the ash heap. He observes the childless woman with the breaking heart.

He raises the poor from the dust, lifts the needy one from the heap. He seats them both with royalty, settles the barren woman in a home of her own (verses 5-9).

Almighty God, majestic Savior, King of the universe—intimately involved in the lives of people—you—me. Who can comprehend His incomparable glory?

We are finite humans, and it's hard for us to grasp truth about our infinite God. Sometimes it's even harder to express that truth and wonder in words because they are so limiting.

God knows this, so in addition to words, He gave us the gift of music. When we sing His own words, resplendent with His glory, back to Him, we become part of a circle of wonder.

Often, when we're with other believers, we do it best. "From you comes my praise in the great assembly; before those who fear you will I fulfill my vows" (Psalm 22:25). Mingling our praises with those of others means we share the heart of God.

How, Then, Shall We Praise Him?

A frustrated Sunday School teacher spread her hands wide. "When I talk about praising God, the kids start thanking Him—for finding their lost kitten, for helping them pass a math test. When I tell them that's good, but that they also need to praise Him for who God is, they just look at me."

Aren't many of us like these children? Pure praise for who God is feels strange on our lips. How should we praise Him?

Barbara Haycraft, in "Learning to Praise" in the *Discipleship Journal* (Issue 38, March 1, 1987) gives these practical and helpful suggestions:

• Do not use the word praise. This will force you to say what you mean without relying on a word that may have a vague meaning for you. The restriction may seem difficult or awkward at first; you may feel that your words lack the luster of expression you wish they had. But as you start to pray what is in your heart, your praises will become more natural and will begin to flow more spontaneously.

• Do not use the word thanks. Praise and thanksgiving are

close but distinct forms of prayer: We thank Him for what He has done; we praise Him for who He is. Thanksgiving is an important part of prayer, but when we are not sure how to praise, it can become a substitute for praise. Eliminating "thanks" from your praise vocabulary will help you focus on true praise.

• Try to begin your prayer sentences with "You" rather than "I." For example, you might say, "You are great and mighty," or "You are the God of compassion and mercy." This will help you not to focus on yourself or your requests. God, not ourselves, is the subject of praise.

A personal praise note:

"Lord Jesus, you are so beautiful. You are the Comforter, Counselor. You are worthy to receive adoration.

"You are the Most High, the Author of all things, Sovereign Lord. You are King in heaven. King right here. You are the Lamb who takes away the sin of the world. There is no one like you. No name like your name."

In Praise of His Name

There is probably no single study that will enrich our praises more than a study of the names of God. God chose to reveal Himself to man from the beginning by introducing new truth about who He was to the people through His Names. He continued through the New Testament where we see Jesus who has been given, "the name that is above every name."

An example of this progression in His names is in the last verse of Ezekiel where God reveals Himself as *Jehovah Shammah, "the Lord is there."*

Ezekiel began his prophecies when Israel was at an all-time low both spiritually and nationally. The golden splendor of David and Solomon's reign was gone; the darkness of captivity was closing in around them. Their spirits were broken.

The Psalms tell us the Israelites sat and wept when they remembered Zion. They hung their harps upon the

93

willows and refused to sing.

Ezekiel's prophecies change from despair to hope. Israel will be restored. God would bless them far beyond anything they had ever experienced. "I saw the glory of the God of Israel coming from the east. His voice was like the roar of rushing waters, and the land was radiant with his glory" (Ezekiel 43:2). Their pledge that this would happen is in the name God gave the promised city—*Jehovah Shammah*, "*Jehovah is there*" (48:35).

This truth hid in the darkness of Jewish history between Malachi and Matthew. Eventually it rested on a tiny baby lying in a shadowed barn. "The virgin will be with child and will give birth to a son, and they will call him Immanuel—which means, 'God with us'" (Matthew 1:23). That baby is the Immanuel of Isaiah (Isaiah 7:14). He is "Jehovah is there," the *Jehovah Shammah* of Ezekiel.

Jesus walks through the Gospel accounts. The disciples fished with Him, slept and ate with Him. But eventually they had to learn to do without those things. Even though Jesus told them He would return to take them to Himself, years without His physical presence stretched before them. They had to learn in a new way that he was *Jehovah Shammah*, Immanuel, God with us.

Jesus said, "But I tell you the truth: It is for your good that I am going away. Unless I go away, the Counselor will not come to you; but if I go, I will send him to you" (John 16:7).

His presence is part of the inheritance promised to us. "For we are the temple of the living God. As God has said: 'I will live with them and walk among them, and I will be their God, and they will be my people'" (II Corinthians 6:16).

A full-blown rose sits on my desk. Several days ago it was a bud of promise—the petals were curled tightly together. Gradually the petals unfurled, releasing aroma, beauty.

The Old Testament name, *Jehovah Shammah* is a tightly-budded flower of life-changing truth. The flower opens in the

New, a baby wrapped in swaddling clothes—God with us.

I turn the pages of my Bible. Revelation 21:22—a crimson rose in majestic fullness. There is no further need of any outward symbol of His presence. "The Lord God Almighty and the Lamb are its temple."

"Now the dwelling of God is with men, and he will live with them. They will be his people, and God himself will be with them and be their God. He will wipe every tear from their eyes" (Revelation 21:3-4).

A Path of Light

We see another unfolding revelation of glory in the Old Testament name, Sun of Righteousness (Malachi 4:2). Zechariah sang about the coming Messiah before His birth. He said, "...The rising sun will come to us from heaven to shine on those living in darkness and in the shadow of death, to guide our feet into the path of peace" (Luke 1:78-79).

John, the disciple closest to our Lord's heart during His ministry on earth, recorded God's testimony of Jesus, the light of the world (John 1:1-9, 8:12). In Revelation, this same John described Him in a vision of light: in the middle of golden lampstands, wearing a golden sash. His hair was as white as snow, His eyes like blazing fire, His feet like bronze glowing in a furnace, His face like the sun shining in all its brilliance. In His hands He held seven stars (Revelation 1:12-16).

Jesus is the Sun of Righteousness, the Light of the World, the Lamb who is the only source of light in heaven. He is the greatest Star of all, unchanging, always there, eternally brilliant.

When Jesus promises to give His faithful ones the bright and morning star (Revelation 2:28), He's promising to give us Himself and all that's inherent in who He is.

An artist once drew a picture of a man alone in a boat on the sea. Waves crest above the man's head. A single star gleams through a rent in the darkened, angry clouds.

The voyager fixes his eyes on the star. Beneath the picture are the words, "If I lose that, I'm lost."

Life is filled with difficulty, darkness—even danger. But music and grace come to us on the waves. The music lifts us higher. "Amazing grace, how sweet the sound...."

Grace lifts us even higher. There is power in praise. There is beauty, too.

A Gift That I Can Bring

One of my most memorable moments came at sunrise. Driving from Sherwood to Wilsonville, I topped Baker's Hill in time to see a sea of gold and pink clouds. I stopped the car and watched the morning sun paint Mount Hood a fiery pink.

A radiance stole into the air as the clouds in the east became feathers of rose and violet. Shades of blue sky accentuated the sunlight slanting onto distant hills. The light slowly advanced, a stand of timber, a field of grain, the car in which I sat.

The beauty of it all moved me like great music. A longing dropped into my heart. Oh, for something as beautiful as this to give to the Lord of glory.

Then I realized, I already have it. Praise is part of the discovery of God Himself. It begins at salvation and continues through eternity.

John records Jesus' last words in Revelation. "I, Jesus, have sent my angel to give you this testimony for the churches. I am the Root and the Offspring of David, the bright Morning Star" (Revelation 22:16).

And then His promise, "Yes, I am coming soon."

Even so, come Lord Jesus. Amen.

FOOTNOTE
[1]Warren Wiersbe, *Real Worship*, Thomas Nelson Publishers. Used by permission.

96

Helps in Setting the Sail:

1. Choose a psalm or a song from the hymnal that expresses your praise to God regarding worship. Think about it through the day. Let it become a song in your heart.

2. Meditate on the sentences beginning with "Worship is..." quoted at the beginning of this chapter. Chart your personal response to God by crafting your own sentence(s): "Worship is..."

3. Begin now to keep a list of the names of God you find in Scripture: Creator, Redeemer, The Lamb, King, Bridegroom, Rock, Refuge, Comforter, Shepherd. Refer to them often as you worship in your quiet time and in the church worship service.

4. Read the worship songs in Revelation (4:8-11, 5:9-13, 7:10-12,15-17, 11:15-18, 19:4-9), then Warren Wiersbe's prayer below. Use them to help you express the praise in your own heart.

Lord, God, I bow in awe of your holy presence.
I am overwhelmed by the thought of your majesty....
Mighty God, I praise your holy name.
    I acknowledge the wonder of who you are,
    what you do on my behalf,
    how you speak to me through your magnificent word.
My personal worship falls short of the desire of my heart—
    yet how grateful I am for my time with you.
Heavenly Father, you have been patient as I have struggled
    in my personal worship.
    You understand my tangled motives;
    the feelings I can't even put into words.
Renew my spirit.
Receive my praise.

Accept my thanksgiving.
  I ask in the name of Jesus Christ my Lord.

Amen

Suggestions for Family Sailing:

1. Give each family member a file card with several names of God written on it. Spend time in praise as each person reads a name. Instruct them to do it slowly so that each person, in the silence that follows, can think about what the name means.

Later you may want to make a statement that relates to the name. This can help your family focus on praise that is God-centered.

Another suggestion is to play a listing game to see how many names of God the entire family can write down. You can use this list later as you praise Him for who He is.

2. Encourage the entire family to memorize favorite Scripture portions that express praise. (Exodus 15:1-2, I Samuel 2:1-2, Psalm 99:1-5, Psalm 112, Psalm 145, Psalm 119:97-104, Habakkuk 3:17-19, Romans 11:33-36, Ephesians 3:20-21)

3. The "light" verses below can help family members trace a path of light through the Old and New Testaments. Copy the acrostic on separate sheets of paper, one for each family member. Half the family does the Old, the other half the New.

(Genesis 1:3)_____ L_____
(Nehemiah 9:12)_____ I _____
(Proverbs 4:18)_____ G_____
(Isaiah 60:1-3)_____ H_____
(Malachi 1:11, 4:2)_____ T_____

(Luke 1:78-79)_____	L_____
(John 1:1-9)_____	I_____
(I John 1:5-7)_____	G_____
(Revelation 1:16)_____	H_____
(Revelation 22:3)_____	T_____

4. Encourage family members to put favorite Bible verses to music. You might even have a family concert. Invite close friends and extended family.

Chapter Nine/
With a Resounding Amen

Saying Amen is saying "yes," to God.
We say "yes" to God...
>When we come to worship.
>When we praise Him in music.
>When we unite our prayers with those of others.
>When we listen to Scripture being read.
>When we bring our offering.

"I think I just want to say thank you," Ken said earnestly. "For years Rosie and I didn't go to church. Oh, we visited here and there. But somehow...."

"Those were hard years," Rosie continued. "Searching— not even knowing we were searching or what we were searching for. I'll never forget the Sunday morning Ken said he wanted to be part of this church. That he wanted to give his tithe."

"When I put our check in the plate," Ken said, "I knew we were committed."

"A joy exploded inside me," Rosie confided. "All those

years there'd been no place to bring my sacrifice—
my offering. No place where I could say *yes* to God."
Ken and Rosie learned a truth that many of us haven't
grasped yet. We're created with a need for a place
to bring our sacrifices, our offerings. A place we can
go and by our very going say "yes" to God.

Saying Yes to God in Prayer

Amen means "to be established, to be faithful, to
be firm." Another way to say it is, "let it be" or "so be
it." Saying amen means we put ourselves under God's
authority. We accept His person, His will, His Word,
and His provision.

We are created to give ourselves to God as spiritual
sacrifices. "Therefore, I urge you, brothers, in view of
God's mercy, to offer your bodies as living sacrifices,
holy and pleasing to God—this is your spiritual act of
worship" (Romans 12:1).

Prayer is a part of this spiritual sacrifice. The psalm-
ist wrote, "May my prayer be set before you like
incense; may the lifting up of my hands be like the
evening sacrifice" (Psalm 141:2).

In Revelation 5:8 and 8:3-4, incense symbolizes "the
prayers of the saints."

Each individual Christian can pray alone, but when
we pray in company with other worshipers, we're stretched beyond ourselves. As we join our hearts to those
who pray in church, whether the pastor or another,
we may be stirred to pray for needs we knew nothing
about—a Supreme Court hearing in process at the nation's
capital—a family without adequate shelter—a marriage in need of restoration—a man or woman in need
of a job.

Praying is part of saying "yes" to God. We do it best
together.

All the People Said, "Amen! Amen!"

Sometimes we forget that reading the Scripture is an integral part of our worship together. When Ezra read the Word to the people, "…the people all stood up. Ezra praised the Lord, the great God; and all the people lifted their hands and responded. 'Amen! Amen!' Then they bowed down and worshiped the Lord with their faces to the ground" (Nehemiah 8:5-6).

There is glory to be seen in the Bible, a glory that surpasses that of creation. God's Word reveals His character and His excellency, the very essence of who He is. His Word reveals His heart.

The Glory of His Word

Psalm 19 begins with creation's song in the heavens. This silent song sweeps to the earth, pouring out non-verbal speech and displaying God's knowledge. In verse seven it bursts into a verbal song of praise to God for His Word.

The Word of God is…

perfect, reviving the soul.
trustworthy, making wise the simple.
right, giving joy to the heart.
radiant, giving light to the eyes.
pure, enduring forever.
sure, and altogether righteous.

Creation reveals God's power and glory, His deity. But only in His Word do we meet Him as a personal God.

His character and His Word move like a majestic two-part symphony through this psalm, through the entire Word of God. "For the word of the Lord is right and true; he is faithful in all he does" (Psalm 33:4).

His Word is the only complete revelation of redemption's glory. "The Word became flesh and made his dwelling among us. We have seen his glory, the glory of the One and Only, who came from the Father, full of grace and truth" (John 1:14).

102

Public reading of Scripture continued into the New Testament. "He went to Nazareth, where he had been brought up, and on the Sabbath day he went into the synagogue, as was his custom. And he stood up to read" (Luke 4:16). When Paul instructed Timothy concerning the ministry the Lord desired for him, he included public Scripture reading (I Timothy 4:13).

Reading the Word is reading back to God what He's already said. This revelation of glory calls us to examine our hearts. It calls us to worship. To say "yes" to Him.

Gifts—Fragrant Offerings—Sacrifice

There's another way we say "yes" to God. Ken and Rosie discovered it when they made a commitment to give a portion of their money to the Lord.

They weren't the first. After Moses talked with God on Mount Sinai, he instructed the people, "This is what the Lord has commanded: From what you have, take an offering for the Lord. Everyone who is willing is to bring to the Lord an offering of gold, silver and bronze; blue, purple and scarlet yarn and fine linen; goat hair; ram skins dyed red and hides of sea cows; acacia wood, olive oil for the light; spices for the anointing oil and for the fragrant incense; and onyx stones and other gems to be mounted on the ephod and breastpiece."

He instructed them further. "All who are skilled among you are to come and make everything the Lord has commanded: the tabernacle...the ark...the altar...garments worn for ministering in the sanctuary" (Exodus 35:4-19). God filled these men with His Spirit to work with skill, ability and knowledge. Craftsmen, artists, weavers, embroiderers—all came willingly.

And the people continued to bring freewill offerings morning after morning—and there was more than enough. The people even had to be restrained from giving.

Our churches are places where people can bring their

103

offerings...the tithe, a monthly check for the building fund, a Sunday School class pledge to provide Christmas gifts to a missionary family.

Libby brings her organizational skills, Al and John their construction expertise. Nan hangs curtains. Keith helps in a preschool class.

The worship leaders lead the congregation in songs and hymns and arrange special music. Teachers teach and pastors preach. Children bring warm welcomes and songs, laughter and praises. They erase blackboards and pass out bulletins.

All have something to give...an arm around the shoulder, a hug...perhaps a tear.

But the church is more than a building and activities. Our bodies are His temple. We go into the world.

Michael and Ellen and Becky and Bill are involved with their local school board. Pat and Judi practice hospitality. Steve and his small band of committed young people bring Jesus into the high schools.

It's significant that the Apostle Paul avoided the word money when he talked about the generosity of those who supported his ministry. Instead, he uses the words gifts, fragrant offering, and sacrifice. These words told the Philippians that in assisting him, they were offering worship to God.

"Through Jesus, therefore, let us continually offer to God a sacrifice of praise—the fruit of lips that confess his name. And do not forget to do good and to share with others, for with such sacrifices God is pleased" (Hebrews 13:15-16).

The Danger of Drifting
Singing, praying, reading the Word, bringing an offering, these may seem like small things, but are they? Danger lurks anytime we do something repeatedly, Sunday after Sunday, week after week, month after month, year after year.

Overexposure even to great revelations of truth can lead to carelessness. Carelessness and neglect are dangerous—they lead to spiritual drifting. The letter to the Hebrews helps us understand.

The first chapter is filled with the radiance of Christ's glory. Phrases like, "appointed heir of all things," "through whom he made the universe," "the radiance of God's glory." "The exact representation of his being," "provided purification for sins" and "sat down at the right hand of the Majesty in heaven," are only a small part of the description given of Jesus Christ.

This chapter sings with the superiority of God's Son and the greatness of His sacrifice for our salvation. It follows with a warning in the opening verse of chapter two: "We must pay more careful attention, therefore, to what we have heard, so that we do not drift away" (Hebrews 2:1).

"Drifting" is a nautical term that speaks of slipping away. William Barclay in *The Letter to the Hebrews* writes, "...This first verse could be very vividly translated, 'Therefore, we must the more eagerly anchor our lives to the things that we have been taught lest the ship of life drift past the harbour and be wrecked.'"

Drifting happens subtly, almost without warning. A job change. Children born. Doctor appointments. Soccer practice. A new motor home. Weekends on the bay...in the mountains...on the lake.

Oh, we don't intend to leave our Lord. We're not denying Him. It's just that....

A careless sailor neglects to properly tie the knots while mooring in what appears to be a safe harbor. A distracted sailor forgets to lower the sail. A careless sailor fails to let down a necessary anchor.

The boat begins to drift. Those on the boat drift with him.

This sailor jeopardizes not only his own life but the crew, the cargo, and even the ship itself. A sand bar, a rocky reef, a sudden storm. All kinds of things can happen to a drifting boat.

It's easy to drift when important things become too familiar...when we've heard something so many times we tune it out. It happens with worship, music, God's Word, prayer. We forget to listen, to acknowledge His greatness. Our minds drift...

We hit a sand bar. Someone doesn't notice how hard we worked on the mission board.

We hit a rocky reef. Our son is caught smoking marijuana. The youth pastor doesn't want to get involved.

We start to drift. Oh, our bodies are in church, but our hearts? Instead of concentrating on Christ, we turn inward. Instead of looking at Him, we look at people. Usually, we don't like what we see.

But the glory of who God is is being revealed in the worship service. Voices sing, "His Name Is Wonderful." Prayers ascend as incense. The Scripture instructs and reproves, opens up the deep down hurting places inside us. Our pastor exhorts, encourages, and comforts.

Our Lord is ready and able to meet us at our point of need. He stoops forward. He listens.

He waits to hear us shout a resounding "Yes!" to Him.

Helps in Setting the Sail:
We say "yes" to God when we pay careful attention to the things we've learned.

1. Bring pen and note pad to church. Be prepared to write down a prayer need you didn't know about before you went. Make a commitment to pray about it during the week.

2. Write down a verse or phrase from the Scripture reading that speaks to your heart. Meditate on it this week.

3. This week may be a good time to evaluate prayerfully (or to reevaluate) what portion of your money God wants you to give for the work of the local church. Do the same with your talents, your spiritual gifts. Verses like Romans 12:1-2, II Corinthians 9:6-15 and Ephesians 4:7-16 can help you focus on what His Spirit wants to say to you.

4. Ask the Lord to reveal to your heart more of the wonder of who Jesus is. Read the first chapter of Hebrews. List each descriptive phrase, then form them into a personal praise song of worship.

Suggestions for Family Sailing:
1. Provide your children with opportunities to read Scripture aloud at home. The occasional use of responsive readings adds interest and variety.

An example of this kind of reading is found in Deuteronomy 27:12-13. Six tribes stood on Mount Gerizim and read God's words of blessing; six tribes stood on Mount Ebal and read words of cursing should they not obey God's Word.

With a little effort, parents and children can develop dramatic readings that are fun and true to God's Word. Rather than alternately saying verses, divide phrases among family members. This type of reading allows the meaning to come through more clearly. It is especially adaptable in the Psalms. From the opening words of Psalm 111:

Father: Praise the Lord.

Mother: I will extol the Lord with all my heart in the council of the upright and in the assembly.

Mike: Great are the works of the Lord; they are pondered by all who delight in them.

Heather: Glorious and majestic are his deeds, and his righteousness endures forever. He has caused his wonders to be remembered;

Tony: The Lord is gracious and compassionate.

Father: He provides food for those who fear him; he remembers his covenant forever.

Mother: He has shown his people the power of his works, giving them the lands of other nations.

Tony: The works of his hands are faithful and just;

All: All his precepts are trustworthy.

2. Encourage further family participation in the Word through prayers that repeat a single phrase at intervals throughout. Note the phrases, "his love endures forever," in Psalm 118:1-5 and 136; "Praise the Lord..." in Psalm 103:20-22.

Prayers like this can also be written to celebrate special family occasions. One family celebrated the arrival of a long-awaited son by choosing the phrase, "For this new baby, Lord, we praise you."

Each family member wrote or said something special about the new arrival.

We thank you, Lord, for the gift of life.
For this new baby, Lord, we praise you.
His tiny toes, his little nose.
For this new baby, Lord, we praise you.
For future joys and sadness, too.
For this new baby, Lord, we praise you.

108

For baseball hats and fishing trips.
For this new baby, Lord, we praise you.
Later they held hands and each person prayed aloud their personal response. The whole family spoke the chosen refrain.

3. It's important for children to know how the family finances are spent. Occasionally sit down with them and explain how much goes where. Show them the check you're planning to put in the offering.
Encourage them to begin putting aside an offering to give as part of their participation in worship on Sunday morning.

Chapter Ten/
With Listening Ears

"How can we be active participants on Sunday morning when we spend most of our time just sitting and listening to a sermon?"

The gentleman with the graying hair and long sideburns shook his head. "Words, words—they go in one ear and out the other."

Those words, overheard in the church foyer, were sincerely spoken by a man active in the leadership of my church. They confirmed what a friend said to me recently:

"I don't think they really mean to be critical of your sermons, Pastor Norm," Geri said earnestly as she submerged communion glasses in hot sudsy water. "Mostly I think it's just that people don't know how to listen. They don't really understand the impact a sermon can have on their lives.

"Just understanding that took me a long time. Somehow it wasn't easy for me to listen to a sermon with the intention of hearing what God wanted to communicate to me. Or even to see how important it was.

"Learning to take sermon notes was a big first step. Now I can explain what works for me, show my notes to lots of people." She smiled. "You know who I mean, Pastor—those with the big sighs and the—'Oh, I just didn't get anything out of the sermon today.'"

She laughed. "Sometimes I even draw my 'funny man' for them. Want to see?"

She wiped her hands and opened the notebook laying on the table. An out-of-proportion stick man smiled up at me.

Help from "Big Ears"

Geri pointed to the figure's big ears and oversized heart. "I use 'Big Ears' here to illustrate what I call the truth path."

She penciled a line from the ears, to the mind, to the heart and then out through the mouth, hands and feet. "Listening is more than merely hearing with our ears. God's words must impact our minds, go down into our hearts, and then come out in our words and actions."

"Sometimes I give them these quotes." She read the lines beneath the drawing. "(Hear)'... is often used for listening to the Word of God with a firm purpose to obey His commands.' That's from *Cruden's Concordance*.

"Martin Luther said this: 'When I declare the Word of God, I offer sacrifice. When thou hearest the Word of God with all thy heart, thou dost offer sacrifice.'

"Then I have them look up and read Romans 10:17. I ask them the same question you once asked me, 'Does this verse refer to the written word?'

"Almost always they give me the same yes answer I gave you. Then I explain it the way you explained it to me, that 'hear' is the proclaimed or preached word of God and refers to the spoken word, not the written."

She closed her notebook and braced her elbows on the table, her chin in her hands. "I honestly think that most of us have little or no understanding of how God feels about the 'preached

111

word of God.' Nor do we realize that preachers are especially near to the heart of God."

"God Had a Son. He Made Him a Preacher."
The person who said, "God had a Son. He made Him a preacher," has captured a truth that humbles and amazes me. If I am to be a preacher who is near to the heart of God, I must look into the Word and see what sort of preacher Jesus was while He ministered here on earth.

Before I can preach I must listen. I need to involve all my senses and let His Words speak truth to my heart.

I turn to "The Sermon on the Mount" (Matthew 5–7). As I read, I picture salt and lamps, and hypocrites in fringed robes on street corners babbling prayers. I smell lilies, notice fish and bread and fruit.

I pay particular attention to Jesus' sermon conclusion (Matthew 7:24-27). The winds have risen and I can almost taste water on my lips. The whirling sand smarts my cheeks and makes my eyes sting. The houses built by the two men creak and groan. Then one of the houses smashes down with a crash that trembles the sand.

I've carefully listened to the words and heart of Jesus' sermon. Now I'm ready to apply it to my life. I can do that best by asking questions.

Question #1. What truth does it convey to me?

The words Jesus spoke were the words of God. The houses the two men built signified two lives. Jesus said His words were the only secure foundation on which a person could build his life.

He made it clear that the only one who would be able to endure the storms of life was the one who built his life, his house, on solid rock. Jesus said that the rock was His Word, the house consisted of doing His Words.

Merely hearing Jesus' words isn't enough. In fact, it's foolish, doesn't make good sense, is even dangerous. Jesus

112

likens it to building on sand. As soon as a storm blows in, the house would collapse, the life of the person who built it would be in shambles. It could even mean death.

Questions #2 and #3 are a bit more personal. But if I'm to apply truth to my life I must ask them.

#2. When will I put that truth into action?

Since His Word is the only sure foundation for living the Christian life, I need to take it more seriously. I need to memorize this parable this month.

#3. How will I do it?

I'll reread these verses each morning in my quiet time. I'll ask my friend, Dale, to check up on me at the end of the month. I'll also pray each day that God will help me to be obedient to what He shows me in His Word.

These questions can be asked by anyone who desires to be an active participator in the sermons they hear. They can keep us from being people who are only mere hearers and not doers of the Word (James 1:22).

An Act of Worship

A true sermon should be an act of God, not the performance of a man. In real preaching, the speaker is the servant of the Word through whom God speaks and works.

John Killinger wrote, "In preaching, the Spirit has a chance to speak most directly to the worshipper."

When we hear God speak, we have to do something in order for His will to be done in our lives. The first sermon Peter preached in Acts 2 illustrates this principle.

Peter urged the people to "listen carefully to what I say" (2:14). Then he proclaimed the words of the prophet Joel and preached Jesus as both Lord and Christ (2:16-36).

When the people saw this Jesus whom they'd crucified as their resurrected Messiah, they were "cut to the heart and said,...'Brothers, what shall we do?'"

Peter's message of repentance, baptism, and the forgiveness of sins resulted in 3,000 accepting Jesus and being baptized. Not only were they added to the church, they became active participants. "They devoted themselves to the apostles' teaching and to the fellowship, to the breaking of bread and to prayer" (2:42).

Warren Wiersbe expresses it well in *Real Worship.*[1] "The purpose of preaching...is to bring the congregation face to face with the living God." He also says, "When preaching is an act of worship, and listening to preaching is an act of worship, people see and hear God and there is an immediate impact on their hearts and minds."

What Should I Listen for in a Sermon?

It's fun to think of the sermon as a journey the preacher and his listeners go on together. If hearts have been prepared, somewhere on that journey they're all going to meet Christ at some point along the way. Each one is going to have it at a different place.

How important is it for each of us to do that? Cal Leman said, "When we catch a glimpse of God passing by, the pursuit of Him will consume us."

Taking notes can actually help us glimpse God as we become active participants in the sermon. Somehow words going into our ears, our minds and hearts, and out through our fingertips become more truly our own. With our hearts and minds involved in writing, we're more likely to be transformed.

Another benefit of taking notes is that we have something in our hands we can take home that will remind us to live our week with our God. When we take the time to read the Scriptures and rethink God's truth, we experience spiritual growth.

During the sermon we may have been prodded to pray, confess, or reflect further on a habit or attitude that needs attention. We may need to be reminded to pray further about the possibility of teaching a Sunday School class or whether or not we should take that new job. Perhaps we're reminded to drop a note to a sick or discouraged friend or call someone who's absent from church. Jotting thoughts like these down help us follow through in obedience.

It has been helpful for some people who use a notebook in their quiet time to place the sermon notes inside it in chronological order. That way they are more alert to truth God is emphasizing throughout the week.

Others prefer to put theirs in a separate section in their notebook. Still others file them, either under topic or in a file labeled with the book of the Bible.

A word of caution: We need to be careful not to get so involved with a sermon's outline and illustrations that we forget the purpose of preaching. The most important thing is what God writes on our hearts about who He is and what He wants us to do, not what we write down on a piece of paper.

Being an active listener enables us to interact with the message God is shaping for our hearts through His messenger and His Word. It helps us to respond in practical ways to the personalized truth God has prepared for us.

Other Suggestions for Listening, Writing and Applying

Think through the following suggestions of what to listen for in a sermon. Be alert to other ideas that come to you and add them to the list.

Listen for...
1. A revelation of *who God is.*
2. Conviction regarding sin. Recognition of something we must do in response to what we hear.
3. A truth we already know but need to be reminded of.
4. A new truth or a deepened understanding of an old one.
5. Direction or confirmation regarding a decision we have made or need to make.
6. A word of comfort or encouragement.

7. Help for a specific personal need.
Use the following to stimulate your thinking and give you additional ideas for note taking. You may wish to improvise, delete, or add to it, according to your preacher's style and your own personal needs.

Write it down...
1. Many preachers put the key principle being taught in the bulletin, others state it at the beginning of the sermon. Look for it. As soon as you find it, write it down.
2. Roman numerals and the A, B, C outline may work well for some note takers but not all. Most people discover they develop more sensitivity to the Holy Spirit by listening for nuggets of truth, sentences that grab attention, and applications that convict, challenge, or encourage.

Writing these down while they're fresh helps them focus more clearly and quickly on what God is saying to them.

Make it personal...
1. Most preachers use the pronouns we and you. Change those to me and I to make them more applicable.
2. Write down the actual questions the preacher asks. Over the years many have developed skill in asking them. Writing them down will help you interact while you're listening and also help you later to think through truth you've heard.
3. Star the most important truth, word, statement, or application you feel God has for you each Sunday. Train yourself to pray over your starred entry during the week. Ask Him to use it to teach you the way you should go.

You may also want to ask Him how you might share that truth with one other person.

Experiment with creative techniques...
1. Personalize your application into a prayer. The following applications are from I Peter 2:4-12.

Example: "Lord, thank you for choosing me to be your living stone. Clean me up. Polish me. Let me be holy, beautiful, useful in my service to you."

2. Use your name to write a personalized dialogue with your Lord.

Example: "How do I, your living stone, fit into the body, your church, right now? Father God, I'd really like to know."

"_____, today I'm simply asking you to hear my Words in verse twelve. Let me cleanse you from your fleshly desires. Let me imprint you with my likeness."

3. Truth can often be visualized in a simple sketch. Even if you have no artistic talent at all, line drawings and stick figures can be meaningful to you.

I think back to that morning in the church kitchen when Geri said preachers were near to the heart of God. She'd gone on to tell me a folk story about a famous Polish concert pianist which she'd read in a magazine.

"They suggested it as a sermon illustration," she explained, "but I changed the application."

Geri's Story

A mother, wishing to encourage her young son in his piano lessons, bought tickets for a famous man's concert. When the night arrived, they found themselves at the front of the concert hall eyeing the majestic Steinway waiting on the stage.

The mother was distracted by a friend and the boy slipped away. Then—the spotlight came on. The mother gasped. There was her little son sitting at the piano bench picking out "Twinkle, Twinkle, Little Star."

Before she could even move, that famous concert pianist moved to the keyboard. Leaning over, he reached down with his left hand and began filling in the bass part. Soon his right arm encircled the child and music swelled. Together, the old master and the young boy played a symphony of splendor.

When preaching is an act of worship and the message is given to God as an offering from the preacher's heart, then God can take that message and bless it far beyond what we can even ask or imagine. God can ignite the offering that each preacher places on the altar.

Sometimes we need to be reminded that preachers are only novices as they seek to communicate to us our Lord's Song. But as they obediently obey, He transforms their sermons into symphonies. From them can come spiritual light, warmth, guidance, and blessing that has power to transform our lives.

How does God speak to us? In many ways. But one direct channel is Sunday mornings when the heart, spirit, and voice of the preacher unites with His Spirit to deliver the Living Word to waiting hearts.

FOOTNOTE

[1]Warren Wiersbe, *Real Worship*, Thomas Nelson Publishers. Used with permission.

Helps in Setting the Sail:
1. Choose a note taking suggestion to put into practice this Sunday.

2. Meditate on God's special promises to those who "hear" His Word (Revelation 1:3, 2:7,11,17,26-29, 3:11-13,21-22).

Suggestions for Family Sailing:
1. Encourage children to participate in the sermon by providing them with paper and pencil. Challenge them to sketch the truth they hear. Spend time sharing the drawings and the impressions received by each family member. Use them as springboards for discussion.

Encourage, shock, or pleasantly surprise your preacher by sharing your pictures with him.

2. The verses in #2 in *Helps for Setting the Sail* are "picture verses" you and other family members can use to design a series of "overcomer" symbols or pictures. Display in a prominent place in your home (refrigerator/bathroom mirror) to remind each of you throughout the week what God promises to do for the one who "hears" God's Word.

Chapter Eleven/
With a Heart that Remembers

Can you remember the first time you met Jesus?

1956. Chillicothe, Missouri. A young teen with sandy hair, red and white striped shirt, and a thin purple belt, sits in a one room church on the other side of the railroad tracks. He looks down at his black and white loafers.

He's here because he hurts. All through grade school and even into junior high he's come here on Sunday morning. It's a safe place to be—comfortable.

He's come today because he misses Georgia—the varsity cheerleader. He'd been dating her for over a year. And now—it's over. Georgia...

The sermon is hell and damnation but the pastor's wife is gentle. She touches his arm, asks him if he wants to accept Jesus into his life.

He nods and they go to the front together. The words the preacher reads to him from the Bible shake his heart. He's lost, on his way to hell. That night he gives his life to Jesus.

No one told him he'd feel like he's floating as he walks back home—that the heavy weight he'd been carrying would be gone—removed. His black and white loafers almost skip as he crosses the little bridge spanning the railroad tracks.

Suddenly he knows. He squares his shoulders, laughs out-loud. Why, he thought he'd been missing the girl he loved. What he was really missing was the love of the Christ who'd died for him. He's forgiven. Saved. He doesn't want to ever forget.

A Time to Remember

I was that young teenager hurrying home across the bridge. The memory of my introduction to Jesus is as sharp and fresh as when it happened. I don't want to ever forget.

I don't need to. Every time I partake of the Lord's Supper I'm reminded of the cross. I remember that He died for me.

There in the upper room, the very night He was betrayed, Jesus took the bread. "And he...gave thanks and broke it, and gave it to them, saying, 'This is my body given for you; do this in remembrance of me.' And in the same way, after the supper he took the cup, saying, 'This cup is the new covenant in my blood, which is poured out for you'" (Luke 22:19-20).

As often as I eat the bread and drink the cup, I remember His death until He comes for me.

There's another upper room I need to remember. I find it in John 20:19-23. The disciples are huddled together in a second story room behind a locked door.

These men had been part of Jesus' ministry for three years. They had listened to His parables and His sermons, walked side by side with Him, seen His miracles. They had anticipated His kingdom and then witnessed His death. Betrayal–fear–their world had crashed in around them. Even though they had heard the cry, "Christ is risen indeed!" they're afraid. They don't know what to do.

In an hour like this, it's natural for thoughts to turn back-ward.

Do the disciples remember...
- water turned into wine?
- a child cradled in their Master's arms?
- a blind man's cry, "I see men as trees walking"?
- the soldier's spear?
- an empty cross, an empty tomb?

It's also natural for thoughts to turn inward. Do the disciples remember...
- quarreling in the upper room?
- His quiet words in the garden, "Could you not watch with me one hour?"
- swords flashing?
- fleeing for fear?
- watching others prepare His body for the tomb?

The communion table is a time to remember who Christ is and what He did while He was on earth. It's also a time of self examination. "A man ought to examine himself before he eats of the bread and drinks of the cup" (I Corinthians 11:27).

God's Word is pictured as a candle searching the innermost corners of a darkened heart so it can be cleansed and transformed into a place of light and beauty (Proverbs 20:27). "Search me, O God, and know my heart; test me and know my anxious thoughts. See if there is any offensive way in me, and lead me in the way everlasting" (Psalm 139:23-24).

Part of celebrating His supper is placing our thoughts under His authority. Jesus said He was the bread of life (John 6:35). He also said, "I tell you the truth, unless you eat the flesh of the Son of Man and drink His blood, you have no life in you" (John 6:53).

Without food and drink, we die physically. Without Jesus, we die spiritually. "Your forefathers ate manna and died, but he who feeds on this bread [Jesus] will live forever" (John 6:58b).

Jesus is teaching us that we must appropriate Him into every part of our lives in much the same way we eat and drink.

The bread we eat becomes a part of us. The fluid we drink permeates our physical bodies. When we accept Jesus Christ into our lives, we appropriate Him in the fullest sense of the word.

A Prayer of Remembrance

Lord Jesus, it's communion Sunday. I'm not ready—except—I'm here.

I don't have the right attitude, the right words. My thoughts are confused.

I'm rather like the disciples, I think. They hid behind a locked door, uncertain, fearful. They weren't ready, but you came.

I'm here at your table, Lord. And that's about all. Just here. Here to remember....

I remember the helpless lambs they used to bring to the temple. Those altars must have been red with blood. I remember and shudder.

Later, you were that Lamb...

I remember that you forgave my sins. Lord, I place myself under that blood. I am your child.

I remember that you established your church. That you chose it to be your body here on earth. I remember how you gave your Spirit to transform it into energizing love.

Lord, teach me again. I forget.

I remember that you're coming again. You're coming for me, for these believers I'm worshiping with today. You're coming for all believers everywhere.

Lord, I love you, adore you. I exalt and magnify you. I praise your name.

Lord, because I come, I can rest in your arms. I can be at peace.

Because you're my Savior, I give you my sins, my failures. Because you're my strength, I give you my weakness, my fears. You are the Bread of Life, the Living Word. You are my

God. In you will I trust.
Lord, I remember.
I remember your body—this body—this local church I'm part of today.

Remembering Together
When we eat the bread and drink the juice together, we accept our oneness with Christ's body, the church. Here there is neither room for cliques nor the solitary hermit. We're all sinners, cleansed by His blood, worshiping the same Lord.

I remember one communion service where blonde, eager Cynthia and Ellen, with the troubled dark eyes, sat close together on the third pew. I knew them and their parents well. Both girls were in sixth grade, but Ellen attended special education classes locally while Cynthia had all the advantages of a private school.

The girls watched intently as I broke the bread. "For I received from the Lord what I also passed on to you: The Lord Jesus, on the night he was betrayed, took bread, and when he had given thanks, he broke it and said, 'This is my body, which is for you; do this in remembrance of me'" (I Corinthians 11:23-24).

One of the men led a prayer of thanks for Jesus' body, broken for the sins of the world. The organ played as the plates holding the broken loaf passed from person to person.

I looked at the girls. They both knew Jesus. But had they understood when I'd explained about the bread and juice? Did they understand the significance of this moment?

I noticed that Ellen's hands were tightly clasped together, whitening the knuckles. A faint vibration disturbed the soft pink of her dress.

Lord, Ellen's afraid. What shall I do?

Ellen took the plate, her fingers trembling as she clumsily broke off a piece of bread. Holding tightly to her own bread, Cynthia reached out and took Ellen's hand.

Ellen's hand stilled. The two girls sat together, their heads bowed, the dark one close to the blonde, their bread pieces cupped between them.

Jesus was in the midst of us. I was sharing this holy moment as I watched two young lives being welded together.

"Take and eat."

My own bread caught a little in my throat as the girls' hands separated. Joy shone out of the dark eyes and the blue as they ate their bread, smiling at each other.

That morning I recognized anew that just as music magnifies praise, so does communion magnify worship.

This is communion, sharing and worshiping together.

A Time to Forget
While communion is a time to remember, it's also a time to forget.

Confession of sins leads from pain to joy. That truth is suggested in Nehemiah 8 as Nehemiah encourages the people with the words, "'This day is sacred to the Lord your God. Do not mourn or weep.' For all the people had been weeping as they listened to the words of the Law" (verse 9). "Do not grieve, for the joy of the Lord is your strength" (verse 10).

"Then all the people went away to eat and drink, to send portions of food and to celebrate with great joy, because they now understood the words that had been made known to them" (verse 12).

Throughout history God has done and is doing new things. His instruction to the Israelites (and to us) is often: "Forget the former things; do not dwell on the past. See, I am doing a new thing! Now it springs up; do you not perceive it?" (Isaiah 43:18-19).

Paul encourages us with these words, "Forgetting what is behind and straining toward what is ahead, I press on toward the goal to win the prize for which God has called me heavenward in Christ Jesus" (Philippians 3:13).

125

There is a time of self-examination and confession. There is also a time to let go, to forget, to step forward into a new day, a new joy, perhaps a new ministry.

Jesus' appearance to His frightened disciples behind the locked door changed fear into joy, weakness into strength. "Jesus came and stood among them and said, 'Peace be with you!' After he said this, he showed them his hands and side. The disciples were overjoyed when they saw the Lord" (John 20:19-23).

Joy—our joy comes when there is nothing between us and our Lord—when we see Him and know that He is beautiful. Christians clothed in Christ's righteousness rejoice (Psalm 132:9). They sing. The song they sing is a new song. It is like the song the elders sing before God's throne—like the song a friend experienced with her daughter as they sat in an alpine meadow overshadowed by towering Mount Jefferson. Together they expressed their own song of worship and the glory they felt from Christ's presence in their lives.

A New Song

"Oh sing unto the Lord a new song; sing unto the Lord, all the earth," chorused creation.

"Let the field be joyful," sang the meadow.

"And all that is therein," whispered each blade of grass, each nodding flower.

Music swirled around us. "Then shall all the trees of the field rejoice," sang the alpine firs, the pine, the spruce. "Let them clap their hands with joy for the Lord of glory."

A rainbow arched across the lake. "Oh sing unto the Lord a new song," chorused the earth. "Sing unto the Lord, all the earth."

"Oh worship the Lord in the beauty of holiness: fear before Him all the earth," sang the rainbow. "Honor and majesty are before Him, strength and beauty are in His sanctuary."

A glorious white cloud pushed up from the horizon. "He

shall come down like rain upon the mown grass. Like showers that water the earth. You water the ridge thereof abundantly. You make it soft with showers; you bless the springing up thereof."

"Give unto the Lord the glory due unto His name," trilled the waters. "Worship the Lord in the beauty of holiness."

The stream's voice rose in rich crescendo. "The voice of the Lord is upon the waters. The God of glory thunders. The Lord is upon many waters! The voice of the Lord is powerful; the voice of the Lord is full of majesty!"

"Sing unto the Lord a new song, sing unto the Lord, all the earth," sang the earth.

"You crown the year with your goodness, and your paths drop fatness," sang the path behind us.

Several deer hesitated at the water's edge, then bounded away, their white tailed banners held high. "The pastures are clothed with flocks," they bleated. "The valleys also are covered over with grain. They shout for joy, they also sing!"

Beth and I sang the words of our God. "And you my flock, the flock of my pasture, are men, and I am your God says the Lord God."

"Oh sing unto the Lord a new song," chorused the earth. "Sing unto the Lord, all the earth."

Then the great white mountain sang while chills ran up my spine. "You shall go out with joy, and be led forth with peace; the mountains and the hills shall break forth before you into singing, and all the trees of the field shall clap their hands!"

There was a hallowed quiet. The trees ceased their moving, the flowers their nodding. Even the stream's voice of eternal praise stilled. It was an electric silence charged with expectancy.

Into that waiting silence I spoke three words, "Thank you, Lord."

Then our Lord's voice resounded from our hearts, His Word, and off the craggy mountain. It echoed from the hills

127

and bounced on the rocks before us. "You that make mention of the Lord, keep not silence. For I have given unto those who mourn, beauty for ashes, the oil of joy for mourning, the garment of praise for the spirit of heaviness!"

His song was like a mighty ocean wave mingled with a strong and cracking wind. "Whom have I in heaven but you?" His creation chorused with us. "There is none upon earth that I desire before you.

"My flesh and my heart fail, but God is the strength of my heart, and my portion forever.

"Sing for joy, O heavens, for the Lord has done this; shout aloud, O earth beneath. Burst into song, you mountains, you forests and all your trees, for the Lord has redeemed Jacob, he displays his glory in Israel" (Isaiah 44:23).

Creation's music mingled with the words of our God—with our own words. His song became our new song.

We remember His death and resurrection until He comes. "Amen. Come, Lord Jesus. The grace of the Lord Jesus be with God's people. Amen" (Revelation 22:20-21).

Helps in Setting the Sail:
1. Do you remember the day of your salvation? Think about that day. Try to capture the place, the moment—the emotions, the joy. Bring your memory with you on communion Sunday. Caution: Not all Christians can remember the exact day of their salvation. But they can still remember moments or instances of pure joy when they've known they've been in the presence of the Lord, when they've experienced forgiveness at a gut level. Those memories need to be recalled.

2. Write your own song or psalm of remembrance before you come to the communion table. Let it become your personal song as you think of Christ's death, burial, and resurrection.

3. Meditating on the events of the crucifixion before communion can help you remember what this celebration means. Allow them to lead you to the resurrection and a new song.

Suggestions for Family Sailing:
1. Write these memory joggers on file cards, one card for each family member: Something to remember; something to forget; a new song to sing. Distribute them after you talk together about what you discovered in this chapter.

Encourage each one to reflect on each point, then write or draw a brief reminder on the card. Slip the card into your Bible on Communion Sunday. It will help you remember.

2. Families need to remember together what God has done. Read Joshua 4. Collect a pile of large rocks. Each person draws pictures or writes incidents on the stones to remind them of what God has done in their individual lives and in the life of their family. One family I know cut up lengths of 1 x 4s and made a woodpile reminder.

SECTION FOUR/
AFTER WORSHIP WHAT?

Chapter Twelve/
Serve Your Family, Your Church Family

The sign, "Enter to Worship, Depart to Serve," has been placed over the exit doors in many churches.

These words say a lot. Each worship experience of each believer is different, but the call to serve is always the same.

Abraham's worship experience under the oaks was unique. So was Hannah's in the temple, Ezekiel's by the river. None were the same, but they all had similar qualities.

Abraham, Hannah, and Ezekiel saw God and responded to Him. Their experiences brought God glory and resulted in transformed lives. All three were empowered to serve their Lord in a unique and beautiful way.

A Man with A Servant Heart
It's hot and Abraham sits in the entrance of his tent under the shade of the great oak trees of Mamre.

Suddenly he looks up. Three figures move across the desert.

He rubs his eyes. Is it a mirage or are these men really traveling in the heat of the day?

Abraham rushes to meet them. When he discovers that his visitors are the Lord and two of His angels, he bows himself to the ground. It is significant that this is the first time the Hebrew word meaning to bow down to worship is used (Genesis 18:2).

Abraham had often worshiped the Lord at the altars he built for Him. Now he ministers to his Lord personally by serving Him a meal.

Three important elements of worship are beautifully illustrated in this man's life. Abraham worshiped. He gave the best that he had to offer to his God—then served his family.

The scene unfolds. Abraham begs the men not to pass on but to allow him to have water brought that they might wash and then rest beneath the trees. He hurries into the tent.

"Quick," he calls to Sarah, "get three seahs of fine flour. Knead it and bake bread."

He runs to his herd and selects a young calf which he gives to one of his servants to prepare. He sets curds and milk and the food that has been prepared before the weary travelers.

This day Abraham, the promised father of nations and man of faith, fetches and carries as he looks after the physical needs of his visitors. He calls himself their servant. He gives the best he has to give.

The scene shifts.

Abraham stands near the tree. As they eat, he's a servant ready and available. A servant, ready to listen, to respond...and now a friend.

Abraham is called a friend of God. What do friends do? Friends listen and talk. Friends look into each other's eyes and exchange the deep things in their heart. What concerns one, concerns the other.

God knew Abraham. He trusted him. Because of this, He shared His heart with him. "The outcry against Sodom and

Gomorrah is so great and their sin so grievous that I will go down and see if what they have done is as bad as the outcry that has reached me. If not, I will know" (Genesis 18:20-21). The men turned and went toward Sodom, but Abraham remained standing before the Lord. Abraham's nephew was in Sodom, Lot's wife, his children.... Abraham begins to intercede for them. God and Abraham are in partnership with one another as Abraham pleads for God to spare his family and the lost sinners of Sodom and Gomorrah. Abraham's worship led him to minister before God and others.

A Woman with a Great Need

Pain—deep down heart pain—drives Hannah to the temple of her God. Her stomach has knotted up; she can hardly eat. Now she bows before her God, pours out to Him her longing for a son.

In Bible times, childlessness was considered a great reproach and a punishment from God. Doubtless, Hannah's pain at not being able to have a baby was intensified because the ultimate dream of every Hebrew woman was that she might become the mother of the promised Messiah.

Hannah recognizes her own inability to do anything about her barrenness. She cries out to God, addressing Him as Lord of Hosts, "The name of the Lord in manifestation of power." The vow she makes reveals she is willing and even longing to give back to God the son she trusts He will give her.

The depth of Hannah's worship and commitment is revealed in her actions. Samuel is born. Hannah stays home to nurse and care for him. When he is weaned, she brings him to the temple, to her God. "So now I give him to the Lord. For his whole life he will be given over to the Lord" (I Samuel 1:28).

The day Hannah releases her son to her Lord, she sings a song of adoration. Hannah sees God as her strong deliverer...

holy as no one else is holy...incomparable...a rock...one who knows all things...a righteous judge...sovereign ruler... powerful Creator...protector...one who fought for her and gave her strength. A practical gift of love flows from Hannah's heart and out through her fingertips. She carefully and lovingly sews a special little garment for her son and brings it to him. She does it every year. It becomes a part of her worship experience as she and her husband go to the temple to offer the annual sacrifice.

A Prophet Who Saw God's Glory

Ezekiel's worship experience was different from both Abraham's and Hannah's. Denied the priesthood that was his by right of birth, he receives another commission—that of prophet of God.

Exiled to Babylon by Nebuchadnezzar, Ezekiel sees God's glory in a remarkable vision as he stands by the river Kebar (Ezekiel 1:3). A windstorm, lightning flashes, brilliant light, heavenly winged creatures, whirling wheels intersecting one another. A sparkling expanse of ice, a sapphire throne, a man....

"I saw that from what appeared to be his waist up he looked like glowing metal, as if full of fire, and that from there down he looked like fire; and brilliant light surrounded him. Like the appearance of a rainbow in the clouds on a rainy day, so was the radiance around him. This was the appearance of the likeness of the glory of the Lord" (Ezekiel 1:27-28).

God gives him a description of the task He has for him, and Ezekiel sits with the other captives, overwhelmed, for a week. He is to be used by God to call a people back to Himself? He is to be God's spokesman?

From the first chapter of Ezekiel to the concluding phrase, "The Lord is there," Ezekiel recognizes God's sovereignty.

God is Lord over all creation, people, and nations. Even history bows to His control.

Called to Serve

Each of these worship experiences was very different. Each person saw a unique facet of who God is—Abraham worshiped Him as his Master and Friend—Hannah as her Deliverer, the One who would fight for her. Ezekiel realized God's sovereignty, majesty, and power.

However, they each received a specific enabling to do a certain task. Abraham was called to intercede for his family's needs; Hannah gave her son back to God, then served him and other family members in practical ways. Ezekiel proclaimed God's word to a rebellious people who would refuse to respond.

God's glory calls us most often as we worship before Him. "His divine power has given us everything we need for life and godliness through our knowledge of him who called us by his own glory and goodness" (II Peter 1:3).

We see His radiance in the lives of godly men and women. How does the knowledge of God change ordinary people into extraordinary servants?

Worship doesn't stop when the last hymn is sung and the last prayer is said. Our worship continues as we walk out the door and jump into our cars, as we interact with our families and penetrate our neighborhoods.

Worship and service are like links of a chain connected together. Worship gives a holy strength that enables us to serve. Service stimulates within us a holy desire to worship God again, on a daily basis, and then together as a body.

Worship and serve. Serve and worship. God uses these worship and serve experiences to build character deep within the hearts of His men and women.

We're challenged by these men and women with whom we worship each week. How does their knowledge of God

137

call them to life and goodness? What difference does knowing Him make in the everyday round of their lives?

God's splendor sparkles from His Word and from the lives of His people as they seek to revere and serve Him. When we experience God's holiness and glory—His forgiveness and power—then we are ready to serve Him no matter how difficult the task.

Our families are good places to begin.

Serving the Family

Charles Swindoll says home is, "Where milk is spilled, where toes are stubbed, and where people see you in your underwear. It's real life" (*The Practical Life of Faith*).

The phrase, "real life," is what makes serving the family so important...and so hard. Jesus understood how difficult it is to minister to our physical families. He said, "Only in his home town and in his own house is a prophet without honor" (Matthew 13:57).

Family can be the most difficult because they see us in our true light; they demand the most from us relationally. They are also the ones who give us the greatest return.

Husbands, wives, and children are usually with us through a lifetime; they are the ones we most profoundly affect. Children grow up and away, but our influence follows them and their children, their children's children—family members are our most important disciples.

Discipling in its simplest definition is two lives rubbing against each other. Families rub hard...but beauty can come from the rubbing, especially when family members know they're loved as "real people."

How then do we love?

We love in many ways. Husbands and wives provide for material needs. Food is provided, floors are scrubbed, meals prepared. Cuts are bandaged and bruises kissed. But there needs to be time to do the "extra thing," that special something that lights up the eyes.

A father was asked how he said, "I love you," to his wife and two small daughters. "I want them to learn the language of love that flowers communicate so I bring each of my girls a rose. I do it every month." He smiled. "My mother told me flowers always say, 'I love you.'"

Dorothy reads *Sports Illustrated* and yells herself hoarse at her son's soccer games. Mandie shares her mother's quiet time once a week at a nearby restaurant.

Tina and Rob backpack with their two sons and daughter. "Tina and I have special times with our friends," Rob said. "It's important for the kids to know they're our best friends."

Serving our families means prayer and discipleship—fun times and hard times. It's life in the real world. Sometimes it hurts.

Serving in the Local Church

Serving the church family can be tough, too, especially when...

- the music is poorly selected, slow, too much.
- the nursery is poorly staffed.
- the Bible study leader drones on and on.
- there's another good church close by, or downtown, or across town.

But the church is more than a building or a series of meetings. It's the body of Christ. Christ is the head; the redeemed children of God are the body. Each person is a vital part of Christ's body.

Church involvement isn't just receiving. We all need activities in which we give of ourselves, a place to come where we can exercise our spiritual gifts and talents.

One of the ways we discover our spiritual gifts is by trying different ministries. Teachers don't learn to teach unless they study the learning process and then actually do it. It's even okay if we fail. How else do we discover our weaknesses and strengths? Our unique place within the body of Christ? Picture God as the Light of the World, you His prism. The unique shape and color of the rainbow from your prism is a reflection of your life—your ministry, personality, talents, environment, heritage, interests, and spiritual gifts—filtered through the presence of the Holy Spirit in your life. Only you can reflect Him as light into a darkened world.

Just as no two prisms reflect the same colors in quite the same way or the same place, neither can one person's ministry be duplicated by another. God has made each of us into a one-of-a-kind person with a one-of-a-kind, God-designed ministry.

But when I look out at the people gathered for worship on Sunday morning, do I see a group of people whose sins and flaws make them act in ways I'd rather not think about? Or do I see them as God does? "And we, who with unveiled faces all reflect the Lord's glory, are being transformed into his likeness with ever-increasing glory, which comes from the Lord, who is the Spirit" (II Corinthians 3:18).

When we unite together, we make a reflection of that greater rainbow in heaven, the one encircling God's throne (Revelation 4:3). We do it as we serve others at home, at church, at work, in the neighborhood.

Putting It Together

But sometimes the church and the family seem to be in conflict with one another. Finding balance between these two can be a little like trying to balance a teeter-totter.

"It's easier for me to be involved in the church than it is for me to serve my own family," Arlis confides. "Often my husband and kids come last of all."

Neil's problem is just the opposite. "We don't have time for the church in the middle of the week," he explains. "On Mondays we have Little League; Tuesdays are family night; Wednesday is soccer....No way are you going to get me out."

Then there's Rhonda. A single parent, Rhonda has some-how successfully integrated her family into the life of the church. Kid's Club is her joy. If you come early that evening, she's likely to be found in the fellowship hall, laying out the evening activities.

She isn't alone. Her three children are with her. Paula fetches boxes from the car. Scott cuts out giraffes and pastes tiny eyes on zebras. Traci helps early arrivals at the registration desk. Rhonda's ministry isn't just "her ministry." Her family is involved and just as excited as she is.

How did it all begin? How does she do it?

"It started the Sunday morning Eileen sang, 'People Need the Lord,'" Rhonda explains. "I looked around and all I could see were children's faces. I knew I had to do something. It seemed like Kid's Club was that something.

"But before I could do anything, I had to be cleansed. I had resentment and bitterness left over from my divorce. I had to give them to Jesus. And I did. Then I was freed to follow the desires the Lord had given me.

"How did I do it? For one thing, the entire family was involved from the beginning. I think if I've done anything right, it's that I've tried never to let church responsibilities make my kids feel I'm too busy for them. They know their needs are every bit as important as the needs of the kids in club. Sometimes they're more important.

"Another thing—we laugh a lot. We laugh on the way to church—at church—at home before we come. We pray to-gether about Kids' Club, too—talk about each one of their various friends—plan fun things to make those friends want to come."

Rhonda and her family are learning that, "The path of the righteous is like the first gleam of dawn, shining ever brighter till the full light of day" (Proverbs 4:18). The light of God's Word shines more and more into her life and the lives of her children with each step of obedience she takes.

Rhonda illustrates that genuine worship is life-changing, not only for herself, but for others. Her family is reflecting the Lord's glory at home, at church, and out into the community.

Helps in Setting the Sail:
1. You and I can experience God's glory as we see Him on the pages of our Bibles (Ephesians 1:18). We can see Him revealed in the lives of other godly men and women whose worship experiences transformed their lives.

Spend time this week observing Isaiah (Isaiah 6:1-8), Jeremiah (Jeremiah 1:4-10), David (I Chronicles 21:16-24), John (Revelation 1:10-19), and Mary of Bethany (John 12:1-8, Mark 14:8-9). Ask God to teach you truth that will transform your personal worship. Use the following questions for insight.
1. How did this person see God?
2. Describe how you think they felt.
3. What was their initial response to God?
4. What happened in each life as a direct result of beholding God?

At the end of the week, note similarities and differences. What did you discover about real worship? In what ways did you identify with each experience?

2. Service flows from worship. This Sunday write down one practical way you can serve each family member during the week. Ask a friend to keep you accountable.

3. Take a look at your own church body. What are the areas of need? How might you fit into one of them?

Suggestions for Family Sailing:
1. Write II Corinthians 3:18 on file cards for each family member to take to church. Encourage them to read the verse and ask the Lord to open their eyes to the beauty in each person worshiping with them. As they observe the diversity in several individuals they already know, they can then picture each person as a different reflection of Christ.

2. Remind them to thank the Lord for the marvelous blending of personalities in your church and to worship Him for His glory and creativity in gathering together these unique multi-colored lights to reflect His glory.

Chapter Thirteen/
Serve Your Community, Your World

After Jesus' resurrection, seven of the disciples gathered by the Sea of Galilee in obedience to Jesus' message spoken to the woman at the tomb, "Go and tell my brothers to go to Galilee; there they will see me" (Matthew 28:10).

They go, but these men are a restless, milling group, lacking purpose, uncertain what to do. There's a tang in the breeze coming off the water that brings back irresistible memories: the feel of the coarse net in their hands, the silver, leaping fish.

Sitting around twiddling his thumbs, waiting for Jesus to appear, isn't for Peter. His decision is quick. "I'm going out to fish."

The others respond, "We'll go with you" (John 21:1-3).

The disciples succumb to the lure of the sea, but that night, they catch nothing.

Jesus knows His disciples. Did He ask them to go to Galilee so they would remember the words He spoke when He'd first

145

called them to ministry? "From now on you will catch men"? (Luke 5:4-11).

The events of Christ's appearance on the shore to His fishing disciples in John 21 are a visual of something they needed to remember.

Early in the morning, Jesus stood on the shore of the lake, but the disciples did not realize that it was Jesus.

He called out to them, "Friends, haven't you any fish?"

"No," they answered.

Jesus was allowing His disciples one last glance at their former lives through an empty fishing net. It would remind them of His words, "Without me you can do nothing." Service done in self-will is always emptiness.

He said, "Throw your net on the right side of the boat and you will find some." That wasn't the way you were supposed to fish! The net was always thrown over the left side of the boat. But when they obeyed, they were unable to haul the net in because of the large number of fish (John 21:4-6).

The full net is a picture of the work Jesus had for them to do after His departure. Through the miracle of the fish, He was demonstrating that with His power they would succeed in the area they once had failed.

As soon as Simon Peter heard John exclaim, "It is the Lord!", he wrapped his outer garment around him and jumped into the water. The other disciples followed in the boat, towing the net full of fish. They weren't far from shore, about a hundred yards, but Peter couldn't wait. When the others landed, they saw a fire of burning coals with fish on it, and some bread. Jesus came, told them to bring some of the fish they'd just caught. Then He took the bread and gave them breakfast.

That breakfast on the shore must have been emotion-packed, especially for Peter. The last time he'd been beside a fire with Jesus close by, he'd warmed his hands. But rather than following through with his brave words of commitment, his tongue had stumbled. He'd denied the Lord three times with cursing.

Now...

When they had finished eating, Jesus said to Simon Peter, "Simon son of John, do you truly love me more than these?"

"Yes, Lord," he said, "you know that I love you."

Jesus said, "Feed my lambs."

Again Jesus said, "Simon son of John, do you truly love me?"

He answered, "Yes, Lord, you know that I love you."

Jesus said, "Take care of my sheep."

The third time he said to him, "Simon son of John, do you love me?"

Peter was hurt because Jesus asked him the third time, "Do you love me?" He said, "Lord, you know all things; you know that I love you."

Jesus said, "Feed my sheep."

Jesus, at last using the weaker word for love that Peter had used, says in effect, "Even if you do not trust your own emotions enough right now to say you have deep love for me, I still want you to feed my sheep."

We see Jesus saying the same thing to us. Our service to Christ should depend, not upon the strength of our subjective feelings, but upon our realization of what He has done for us. He accepts us as we are, with whatever we have to give to Him—no matter how small or weak it seems to us, no matter how big our fear or self-doubt.

"I'm Going Fishing."

I think back on Peter—disappointed, tired, weary, ready to go back to the world. That night he catches nothing.

My heart responds as I remember Jesus' words, "Peter, feed my sheep. Peter, feed my lambs. Peter, feed my sheep."

Sometimes when I'm tired or the phone's been ringing with others' pain, and now I'm at home in the yard, trying to start the lawn mower, the Lord and I talk together. Only this time I start the questions.

"Lord Jesus, do you love me?"

My Lord says, "Norm, you know I love you."

I reach for the gas can and stumble over the dog. She yelps. I say, "Lord Jesus, do you really, really love me? Right now, right where I am?"

"You know I do, Norm. Feed my sheep."

"Do I have to, Lord? I'm so tired and your sheep, your lambs, are so hard to be with sometimes. They're so frustrating and unteachable—"

"Norm, do you love me?"

"Lord, you know I love you."

"Then feed my sheep, my lambs."

Joy trembles through my weariness. My Lord wants *me*, a weak and inadequate servant, to be His teacher of those He's entrusted to my care. Those in my family. Those in my church.

First and II Peter are the fulfillment of the commission given to Peter by Christ at the time he betrayed Him, "When you have turned back, strengthen your brothers" (Luke 22:32). Jesus knew Peter's denial was not permanent.

Nor are our failures.

Strengthening the brothers means teaching, discipling, encouraging, praying, caring, helping. It is part of our job description as Christians.

The Chief Shepherd

The words Jesus used to minister to Peter on the seashore were never forgotten by Peter. The epistles prove that Peter faithfully used the principles his Chief Shepherd taught him that memorable night.

I picture Peter on his knees, laying the burdens of the shepherd ministry entrusted to his care before his Chief Shepherd. He asks for specific direction...whispers, "Jesus, what would you have me to do?"

Were his prayers mingled with tears for those who had no Shepherd? His words in II Peter 3:9 communicate deep love. "The Lord...is patient with you, not wanting anyone to perish, but everyone to come to repentance." Peter has been shown the heart of God, now He sees the coming judgment. Did his hand tremble as he wrote the verses that follow: destruction...a world melting with fervent heat...the heavens disappearing with a roar?

He appeals to us, "Since everything will be destroyed in this way, what kind of people ought you to be? You ought to live holy and godly lives" (3:11).

There is no greater privilege than to be partners in ministry with the Lord Jesus Christ. While here on earth we are high priests, anointed servants of the church, His body. We are His heralds, proclaiming the news of salvation to friends and neighbors who do not have our hope.

One day an even greater ministry will open for those who serve Him. They will worship in heaven where Jesus reigns. For "the lamb at the center of the throne will be their shepherd" (Revelation 7:15-17).

The Oil of Joy
"I've been hurting so much," Geri confided. "I've needed the oil of joy in my life. Needed it so badly. I got out my concordance. I discovered in Hebrews 1:9 that Jesus was anointed with the oil of joy. Even His Name, Messiah, means Anointed One!"

"Go on," I encouraged.

"Jesus is God's High Priest. And priests are to be holy, set apart for God's service. I'm sanctified and set apart as His holy instrument of service, too. Joy comes as a result of worship. Joy and victory.

"Fragrance, too. Just this morning I read 'Thanks be to God, who always leads us in triumphal procession in Christ and through us spreads everywhere the fragrance of the knowledge of him'" (II Corinthians 2:14).

"Fragrance? What does fragrance have to do with oil?"

"The anointing oil used to set apart priests and kings was mixed with sweet smelling spices. When I read that, something holy dropped into my heart. Plants used for spices had to be crushed before the oil came forth.

"We're not to be impervious to one another. We're to draw close to each other, be crushed. The result–fragrance–sometimes pain. But giving to others results in joy."

The fragrance of Christ reaches into the world–through us. "For we are to God the aroma of Christ among those who are being saved and those who are perishing. To the one we are the smell of death; to the other, the fragrance of life. And who is equal to such a task?" (II Corinthians 2:15-16).

A Pineapple Upside-Down Cake

Someone has said, "Listen to the music of the gospel." Our lips speak the words, but our actions are the music. And music speaks to the heart.

We are to be sent ones, "the ones with beautiful feet" (Isaiah 52:7). To be sent means we must go to where the hearers are.

Jesus modeled this principle when He, "became flesh and lived for a while among us" (John 1:14). It is revealed in His prayer to His Father, "As you sent me into the world, I have sent them into the world" (John 17:18).

He demonstrated it when He commissioned the seventy-two. "Go! I am sending you out like lambs among wolves" (Luke 10:3).

You and I are sent, too, even if it is simply across the street to the single mom trying to find a babysitter, to the young man sacking groceries at the supermarket.

Jesus spent time with sinners. He ate with them, talked to them, and answered their questions. He taught them.

Relationships are the work of the gospel. They take time. One of the ways we make Christ visible is by reaching out, one friend to another. It might mean a golf game, mowing a lawn, bringing a warm pineapple upside-down cake to a new neighbor. It may mean offering our home to a child after school.

The results of this kind of love outside the body of Christ are evangelistic. Once we build a relationship with someone it's natural to share our Best Friend with that person. Our visible love becomes audible words, building bridges from one heart to another. And as we do, we offer worship to our God for who He is in us—who we are because of Him.

On the Mountaintop
Then the eleven disciples went to Galilee, to the mountain where Jesus had told them to go. When they saw him, they worshiped him; but some doubted.

Then Jesus came to them and said, "All authority in heaven and on earth has been given to me. Therefore go and make disciples of all nations, baptizing them in the name of the Father and of the Son and of the Holy Spirit, and teaching them to obey everything I have commanded you. And surely I will be with you always, to the very end of the age" (Matthew 28:16-20).

Christ stands on the mountaintop, blue sky above Him, brown earth beneath His feet, a picture of authority and sovereignty in both heaven and earth. "When he had led them out to the vicinity of Bethany, he lifted up his hands and blessed them" (Luke 24:50).

This gesture of blessing was something the high priest did after finishing the sacrifice.

Jesus is our anointed Messiah and High Priest. His sacrifice for our sin was accepted by His Father. His blessing speaks of peace, power, and great joy.

"While he was blessing them, he left them and was taken up into heaven. Then they worshiped him and returned to

151

Jerusalem with great joy" (Luke 24:51-52). And they praised God.

The cloud received Him out of the disciples' sight and into the Father's presence–the Lord Jesus Christ, Lord of all, the *Adonai* of the Old Testament, the Master of the New, the King of kings of Revelation.

The Unfurling Rose

God reveals Himself through His Word. We glimpse something of who He is in the Old, then understand more as we look at Jesus in the New. Understanding comes like the gradual opening of a rose; the full glory of who He is is revealed in Revelation.

Our Lord is the *Jehovah Shammah, Immanuel*, the baby in the manger. In Revelation He is the God who dwells with us in our eternal home forever and ever.

He is our Refuge, our Stronghold, our Rock. He is the Word who covers us with the protection of His blood. He is the tent spread over His people.

He is the Sun of Righteousness, the Light of the world, the Lamb who is the light of our future home.

He is the Great I AM of the burning bush. The One who said, "I AM the way, the truth and the life; I AM the resurrection. I AM everything you need."

His names and attributes interfold, blend together, and become One: "One God and Father of all, who is over all and through all and in all" (Ephesians 4:6).

This unfolding of who He is brings joy to our hearts. It's a part of our worship, our service–a gradual process, but through it, we're made beautiful.

His parting commission to His disciples belongs to us too: "Go and make disciples of all nations, baptizing them in the name of the Father and of the Son and of the Holy Spirit, and teaching them to obey everything I have commanded you" (Matthew 28:19-20).

An Ever-Widening Circle

The great commission spurred the disciples to action. What began in Jerusalem reached out in an ever-widening circle that would eventually embrace the world.

This reaching out began as the church worshiped and fasted before the Lord. The Holy Spirit said, "Set apart for me Barnabas and Saul for the work to which I have called them" (Acts 13:2).

While Paul and Barnabas worshiped that day, God transformed them into missionaries. Their commitment to know God and worship Him turned the world upside down. "The two of them, sent on their way by the Holy Spirit, went down to Seleucia and sailed from there to Cyprus. When they arrived at Salamis, they proclaimed the word of God" (Acts 13:4-5).

Real worship is life-changing, not only for ourselves but for others. It is humbling when we recognize that we're on God's team, working together with God to change eternity in someone's heart.

But how can we be part of God's team if we're housebound, family-bound, business-bound?

Our lifestyle change can begin with prayer like the disciples' did in the upper room.

God has ways of burdening believers who are tender toward His goals and desires. He can give each one of us a special place in the world to pray for. He does it just as surely as He gives each believer a specific task within the church.

"I've prayed for the church in Russia ever since Pastor Carl shared from the pulpit the needs of believers in the little town of Gorky," Geri said. "He gave us the names of those who'd been sent to prison because of their faith. One of them was a pastor. That was almost ten years ago, but I still remember him writing their names on an overhead and asking us to pray."

She laid a study guide on the table. "Now, I'm being sent to Austria to help write curriculum that will be used to strengthen the ministries of pastors and church leaders in six

153

countries–East Germany, Poland, Czechoslovakia, Hungary, Romania–and Russia. Do you suppose that what I write might go to Gorky? Strengthen the very people I prayed for?"

I couldn't answer her question. But one thing I did know. Geri has offered herself to be part of the answer to the prayer she prayed so many years ago. The words she's been given to write will follow her prayers into a land she never dreamed she'd go.

Set Sail...

An unidentified quote in a newspaper column states, "A ship in the harbor is safe...but that is not what ships are for." God never intended us to be moored in a harbor with tightly furled sails. We're created to run with the wind. To open ourselves up to His Spirit, to pray, to give, to go.

Jesus' last invitation to the world is "Come." We, the church, His bride, join in the invitation, "Come!"

"And let him who hears say, 'Come!' Whoever is thirsty, let him come; and whoever wishes, let him take the free gift of the water of life" (Revelation 22:17).

Our Lord Jesus wants us to be full partners with Him. We have His promise: "And surely I will be with you always, to the very end of the age" (Matthew 28:20).

Our God is a glorious God. And we were created to worship Him.

Helps in Setting the Sail:
1. Be ready to be part of the answer to your prayer for an unsaved friend or family member. Write the plan of salvation by explaining John 1:12, 3:16, Romans 3:23, 5:8, 6:23, 10:13. Memorize it so you are ready at all times to give anyone who asks, the reason for your hope.

2. Ask God to burden your heart for a particular tribe, people, nation, or individual. Begin to pray daily for those people and for those who may already be ministering to them.

Suggestions for Family Sailing:
1. Help children understand that there are only two destinations for human beings—heaven or hell. Compare them by reading II Thessalonians 1:8-10 and Revelation 21:1-4,8. Encourage them to draw contrasting pictures of the two places by providing large sheets of construction paper and felt-tip pens.

2. Plan a mission evening with the theme, "Like cold water to a weary soul is good news from a distant land" (Proverbs 25:25). You'll need a world map or globe, writing paper, envelopes, and the various addresses of missionaries. Each person chooses a missionary to write "good news" to and shows other family members where they are located on the map. Pray for each missionary family after the letters are written.
Tip: Children will be most interested in missionaries with children close to their own ages.

3. Giving for missions can become a family project as everyone is encouraged to put loose change into a large bank for a designated missionary for a designated time. Make arrangements with your church leaders for the family to place

the bank on the altar, pulpit, or podium.

4. Have each family member write out a prayer of worship as it relates to each one's purpose for living.